BUSINESS ISSUES, COMPETITION AND ENTREPRENEURSHIP

FINANCIAL WELLNESS IN THE WORKPLACE

BEST PRACTICES AND FINANCIAL PLANNING BASICS

BUSINESS ISSUES, COMPETITION AND ENTREPRENEURSHIP

Additional books in this series can be found on Nova's website under the Series tab.

Additional e-books in this series can be found on Nova's website under the e-book tab.

BUSINESS ISSUES, COMPETITION AND ENTREPRENEURSHIP

FINANCIAL WELLNESS IN THE WORKPLACE

BEST PRACTICES AND FINANCIAL PLANNING BASICS

WILFRED O. HUNT
EDITOR

New York

For permission to use material from this book please contact us:
Telephone 631-231-7269; Fax 631-231-8175
Web Site: http://www.novapublishers.com

Library of Congress Cataloging-in-Publication Data

ISBN: 978-1-63463-179-2

Published by Nova Science Publishers, Inc. † New York

CONTENTS

PREFACE

Chapter 1 - In the wake of the recession, many employers have seen how financial distress reduces worker productivity, increases absenteeism, and undermines employees' health. Forward-looking employers have begun to take action, adopting creative approaches to enhance employee financial well-being. Innovative companies are leveraging technology, peer-to-peer relationships, and other promising practices to find low-cost, high-impact ways to promote financial wellness at work. This report is a resource for employers, non-profits, and others interested in promoting financial wellness programs in the workplace.

Chapter 2 - The President's Advisory Council on Financial Capability (PACFC) believes that the workplace offers a critically important and trusted delivery point for financial education and related benefits, with the potential to positively impact as many as 138 million Americans.

Chapter 3 - The President's Advisory Council on Financial Capability was created to advise the President and the Secretary of the Treasury on ways to assist the American people in understanding financial matters and making informed financial decisions. It is tasked with suggesting ways to coordinate and maximize the effectiveness of existing private and public sector efforts and identifying new approaches to increase financial capability through financial education and access to products and services.

One of the Council's areas of focus is enhancing the financial capability of America's workforce. The Council approved a recommendation in January geared toward improving financial capability for federal employees. We have now turned our attention to the private sector, and we hope to inspire employers across all industries to join us in this effort.

We seek to encourage employers of all shapes and sizes to adopt basic financial capability elements—and if they are already so engaged, to step up their offerings to more advanced services. These include a combination of benefits, educational resources, products and services, motivating communications, and metrics for measuring outcomes.

In its May 2012 white paper, "Every American Financially Empowered: A Guide to Increasing Financial Capability Among Students, Workers and Residents in Communities," the White House included a one-page "Employer Checklist" of steps employers can take to improve the financial capability of their employees. The Council's Partnerships Subcommittee has developed an implementation framework to supplement the White House publication in order to more fully support and expand financial capability opportunities in the workplace.

"Financial Capability at Work: A Strategic Framework to Guide Employers" ("Framework") was developed over the past year with significant input from business leaders, employee groups, union leaders, researchers, policy experts, government and nonprofit leaders, human resources and benefits experts and many others. This early guidance took the form of numerous phone interviews and discussions, listening sessions and informal meetings. The PACFC used the input to shape an initial draft document. This draft was publicly released through more than 300 stakeholders for additional feedback and input from September through mid-October, 2012. Thirty-four executive-level stakeholders responded to the following questions:

- Are these elements realistic and achievable for employers to implement?
- What would motivate or inspire your organization to adopt these elements?
- Are there best practices you can share? Are there challenges?

This report provides a high-level summary of that feedback, grouped by key themes. The detailed feedback will be made available on the U.S. Department of Treasury's website.

Chapter 4 - Knowing how to secure your financial well-being is one of the most important things you'll ever need in life. You don't have to be a genius to do it. You just need to know a few basics, form a plan, and be ready to stick to it. No matter how much money you have, the important thing is to educate yourself about your opportunities. This publication covers the basics on saving and investing.

In: Financial Wellness in the Workplace
Editor: Wilfred O. Hunt
ISBN: 978-1-63463-179-2

Chapter 1

FINANCIAL WELLNESS AT WORK: A REVIEW OF PROMISING PRACTICES*

Consumer Financial Protection Bureau

MESSAGE FROM RICHARD CORDRAY

Director of the CFPB

The Consumer Financial Protection Bureau is the nation's first federal agency whose sole focus is protecting consumers in the financial marketplace. The Dodd-Frank Wall Street Reform and Consumer Protection Act also authorizes us to develop and implement initiatives to educate and empower consumers so they can make better and more informed financial decisions. Our job is not only to make the marketplace safer, but also to help people build the skills they want and need to improve their financial lives.

Financial education is central to this mission. If we expect consumers to be responsible for the choices they make, we must support them in developing the skills and knowledge they need. Our strategy to increase people's financial literacy and financial capability includes providing tools and information to help people navigate these decisions, collaborative initiatives with our partners to help us reach consumers, and foundational research to identify, highlight, and spread effective approaches to financial education.[1]

* This is an edited, reformatted and augmented version of a report issued August 2014.

This leads us to focus on financial education in the workplace, where people make some very important financial decisions. At work we may decide how much to save for retirement, whether and how to secure health and life insurance, and whether to set aside funds to meet child care and medical expenses through specialized savings accounts. As more employers give employees the ability to split their paychecks automatically into savings, investments, and checking accounts, the workplace is also helping us set aside money for college, a new car, or a rainy day.

Given this natural connection between the workplace and certain key financial decisions, some employers are already playing a critical educational role for their employees. We are pleased to be reporting here on some of their promising practices and policies. The evidence is preliminary as yet, but some of the initial research on financial education in the workplace already suggests that a financially capable workforce is more satisfied, more engaged, and more productive for their employers.

In this report, we specifically describe financial wellness efforts at five companies: Nebraska Furniture Mart, health care provider QLI, Staples, Goodwill of Central Texas, and Pacific Research. Each of these companies is innovating in financial wellness efforts and finding value in reducing and addressing the negative effects of financial stress on employees. They all took the time to share with us their best practices, and we appreciate their input and believe other employers could adapt and learn from their ongoing initiatives. We also highlight one particular public-private partnership that is operating effectively at scale to support employers and help them take action: Delaware's "Stand by Me" program. State and local officials would do well to consider how they can adapt or replicate the benefits of this program in their own jurisdictions.

Forward-looking employers are already playing an important role in shaping a better future for their employees and our country. We intend this report to spark important discussions about how we can help American workers improve their financial security by developing the financial skills they need to build a better life for themselves and their families.

Sincerely,

Richard Cordray

1. INTRODUCTION

American consumers have come through the Great Recession feeling uneasy and financially insecure.[2] Many, if not most, families say they live paycheck to paycheck. [3] A majority consider their financial situation to be "only fair" or "poor."[4] At night many Americans ponder how to make ends meet. They worry over children, relatives, and friends who have lost jobs. When morning comes, these same Americans take their places in factories and offices where they are expected to do their best to compete across a global economy. But these workers don't leave their money worries at home.

Seven out of ten American workers say financial stress is their most common cause of stress, and almost half (48%) say they find dealing with their financial situation stressful. [5] If an emergency strikes, American workers and their families also have few resources to fall back on. According to the 2012 FINRA Investor Education Foundation's National Financial Capability Study, the percentage of people with an emergency fund of at least three months of savings increased five points between 2009 and 2012. [6] That is good news, but the challenge remains that 60% of households still have less than three months of savings on hand.[7] The Great Recession may have elevated readings of financial stress, but the problem is not new. Even when the economy was booming, financial stress was sapping the productivity and hurting the health of millions of American workers.[8]

This review is intended to serve as a resource for employers who are interested in promoting employee financial well-being by helping their employees develop the skills to better manage their money. Section One introduces the need for financial education in the workplace. Section Two offers an overview of research findings in the field and a discussion of the costs to employers. Section Three presents case studies of some financial wellness practices that employers have found helpful and which might be useful to other companies interested in promoting financial wellness. The report also notes promising trends such as an increased focus on developing employee emergency savings.

Judging by recent surveys, the timing is right for this review. The human resources consulting firm Aon Hewitt polled more than 400 companies in 2014 and found three out of four are somewhat or very likely to expand employee benefits designed to promote financial well-being.[9] Twenty-five percent are likely to assist employees in developing the skills needed to budget and manage their money.[10] Financial wellness programs are not something employers are promoting just because they want to be good corporate citizens, though many do. Large and small employers are beginning to think about financial wellness programs at work because it makes business sense to do so. In an economy where so many employees are stressed about money, providing talented workers with tools to address that stress can be a competitive edge.

Financial Stress and Work

Multiple surveys offer ample evidence of the impact of financial stress at work.[11] For example, in 2012, roughly one in five employees admitted they had skipped work in the past year to deal with a financial problem.[12] Among workers now in their 30's and 40's – a critical cohort of the American workforce - stress levels are even higher. Many Generation X workers (29%) say their personal finances distract them at work, and a majority (53%) find it stressful to deal with their personal finances.[13] This is a particularly salient finding given that Gen Xers – those born between 1964 and 1980 – are beginning to enter their peak-earning years.[14] If they are financially stressed now, Gen Xers may have more difficulty than other generations finding security in the future. Across workers of all generations, 24% admit their personal finances have been a distraction at work. And, of those workers who are concerned about their finances, 39% spend at least three hours each week either thinking about or dealing with financial problems at work.[15]

Given the high levels of self-reported distress, it shouldn't be a surprise to learn that many employees (40%) say that they want help in achieving financial security.[16] And that number is much higher (81%) for workers saying financial problems have affected their productivity.

It's not just employees who want help managing financial stress at work. Managers confront this stress every day. In a recent survey, 61% of human resources professionals say financial stress is having some impact on employee work performance.[17] Twenty-two percent say worries over personal finances have a "large impact" on employee engagement.[18] A clear majority of employers (57%) also say that they believe that financial education boosts productivity.[19]

Despite the challenges financial issues present for employee engagement, Gallup found only 6% of employees strongly agree their organization does things to help them manage their finances more effectively.[20] Given the huge investment employers make in health and retirement benefits that are central to financial security and long-term money management, it is surprising so many employees give their companies low marks on the related issue of helping with financial management.

These findings suggest there is a real opportunity for employers to leverage existing investments in benefits and to reimagine program delivery to enhance employee financial well-being. Some employers are already adopting innovative approaches to address the issues they see among their employees. For example, the office-supply company Staples is using vampire-themed games to make planning for retirement and money management more appealing to busy associates. Other innovative practices identified in this report include programs to reinforce basic money management skills, measure financial stress, and help employees avoid high-cost credit.

Financial Wellness Defined

What do employers mean when they talk about promoting financial wellness programs? There is no single, agreed-upon definition, but there are some common characteristics that surveys, researchers, and companies use in practice.

Financial wellness is a comprehensive approach. Industry surveys define financial wellness programs as those that assess and support an employee's "complete financial picture" or the "overall financial health of an individual." The distinction here is that financial wellness programs do not take a snapshot approach, focusing on a single aspect of financial planning such as retirement or college savings. Financial wellness programs look at how all the pieces of an individual's financial life fit together.

The end goal of a financial wellness program is to enhance the employee's overall financial well-being. That's why financial wellness programs most often support an employee's ability to manage both short-term and long-term needs. Definitions of financial wellness stress the importance of striking a balance between planning for immediate needs while also taking into account long-term goals. As one financial planning firm put it, "financial wellness is . . . the ongoing practice of striking a balance between living responsibly today and planning wisely for tomorrow."[21] The focus is not just on creating a plan, but on enabling employees to make decisions to manage a plan over time.

Financial wellness program assessments may include subjective and objective measures of an employee's satisfaction with his or her personal finances. Objective measures of employee financial status could include assets, homeownership, credit score, debt burden, and the level of emergency savings. More subjective measures are self-reported stress levels and "satisfaction and dissatisfaction with . . . personal financial wellness status."[22] Some definitions of employee financial well-being broaden the subjective and objective factors to consider an individual's "access to resources" and financial health in a social "financial and economic context."[23]

Financial wellness programs take the view that employee financial well-being is influenced by knowledge, skills, and actions that support better financial outcomes. Therefore, financial wellness approaches stress the importance of knowing about "financial concepts and tools" and acting on that knowledge to plan, save and invest.[24] The definitions suggest that financial wellness programs should closely connect education focused on general financial education with opportunities to practice financial planning and implement financial decisions.[25] In this sense, financial wellness programs are as much about learning to do it right as learning the right thing to do.

Approach for This Report

This report explores issues common to many employers and employees who are interested in expanding financial wellness programs in the workplace. It is not designed to be a complete or definitive review of best practices. Rather, it draws on a range of views from research materials, press reports, and discussions with leaders in the field on practices that might be useful for employers to consider offering for their employees.

In developing this report, the CFPB reviewed research literature and industry surveys on financial wellness programs and the delivery of financial education in the workplace. The Bureau also engaged with executives in the private sector, leaders at non-profits, and practitioners in the field of financial education who offered their observations on the development and delivery of financial wellness programs. Several participants in such programs also offered their personal experiences with financial wellness programs.

The executives and employees who offered their time and thoughts come from companies that vary in size from relatively small employers to global competitors. The views presented here provide a range of practical experience and insights. Most importantly, we hope this information will be useful to others considering ways for employers of all sizes to support employee financial well-being.

2. The Business Case for Financial Wellness and the Opportunity for Employers

The increasing focus on financial wellness in the workplace is, in many ways, a natural evolution of programs employers have developed over many decades to support the physical and mental health of their employees. Many employers have folded their Employee Assistance Program (EAP) efforts into health wellness programs, and some have expanded the range of EAP support to include financial counseling for employees who run into trouble managing their credit and debt or face a short-term crisis.[26] The recent financial crisis and mounting evidence that most Americans are ill-prepared for retirement have prompted more employers to expand the wellness approach to include financial wellness, though the terms "financial well-being," "financial fitness," and "financial health" are also sometimes used. [27]

Although there are many definitions of financial wellness, employers appear to take an approach similar to health wellness programs. After initial assessment – either formal or informal – employees participate in counseling or classroom instruction that promotes positive, basic financial behaviors that benefit both employee and employer: budgeting and money management skills, debt reduction, credit score management, and financial goal setting such as increasing savings.

The wellness model offers employers an opportunity to address financial concerns in the context of an existing structure that requires limited additional expenses. Roughly half of all employers already offer wellness programs promoting physical or mental health.[28] The return on investment to employers from comprehensive health wellness programs, though hard to pinpoint, appears to be large, ranging from $1 to $3 or more per dollar invested.[29] If, as some early evidence suggests, financial wellness programs are as effective as health wellness in changing employee actions, companies may see similar benefits from increased productivity and savings associated with reduced sick leave and disability and workers compensation costs.[30]

2.1. Financial Stress and Employer Costs

As noted earlier, financial stress is often cited as a distraction from work and a factor that reduces productivity and engagement. But there is reason to consider whether financial stress may also raise employer health care costs, specifically, the documented link between psychological stress and physical health and well-being. To be sure, it is not easy to define and measure stress with precision. Researchers have also found that the connections between self-reported stress levels, life events, and health outcomes are, to say the least, complicated. Even so, studies have documented the way in which stress reduces the body's ability to fight off disease and increases the risk of premature death.[31] Further, while there is little research on the connection between financial stress specifically and employer health care costs, researchers have attempted to quantify the overall cost to employers from all forms of stress, and they have found those costs are not trivial.

The American Psychological Association has been conducting its "Stress in America" survey since 2007. A 2014 online poll of 1,950 adults conducted by Harris Interactive found money is the top source of stress for the nation, cited by 71% of respondents. That is closely followed by work (69%) and the economy (59%).[32] Another way to look at these results is that the top stress factors all converge in the workplace. Employees are paid at work and they make many of their most important financial decisions at work. Employees also experience the economy through the ups and downs of their employer. The 2013 *Stress in America* results are not an isolated finding. Americans have named money their top source of stress for the last six years in a row and for seven of the last eight years. The *Stress in America* findings follow decades of study examining psychological stress (particularly the link between stress and physical health) that indicates that individuals ranked financial events as some of life's most challenging and stressful events, in some cases ranking ahead of the death of a close friend or trouble with a boss.

Surveys also provide evidence that the stress Americans experience from high debt levels are associated with adverse health outcomes. A 2008 AP-AOL survey of 1,002 adults by Abt SRBI found those who report high debt stress are much more likely to report they suffer from headaches, severe depression, anxiety, and digestive tract problems. While 31 percent of adults with low levels of debt stress say they experience muscle tension and lower back pain, just over half of those with high debt stress experience this kind of pain. High debt stress is also associated with trouble sleeping and concentrating.[33]

In addition to the AP-AOL findings, researchers at Ohio State surveyed 9,200 people between 2005 and 2011 to learn more about their stress levels. The findings of the Consumer Finance Monthly surveys indicate one in five people report debt stress has had a high negative impact on their health.[34] Judging from the available survey evidence, a large share of the American population reports they suffer from chronic financial stress, and they blame that stress for hurting their health.[35]

A recent report in Health Affairs analyzed the health risks and medical expenses of more than 92,000 employees over a three-year period.[36] Those reporting high stress were $413 more costly per year on average than workers who were not at risk from stress. By comparison, smoking – a common health risk targeted by corporate wellness programs – was found to raise health care costs by $587 dollars on average.[37] Since financial problems are an important stress factor, it appears employers may be paying a high cost for employee financial stress, but they do not recognize it because a large portion of that expense shows up indirectly as a health care expense.

The Health Affairs study was careful to point out that their analysis did not measure whether employers can save money by implementing wellness programs, but the authors suggest "such inferences are reasonable, however, in light of abundant medical literature and recent worksite studies that have documented cost savings from risk-reduction efforts."[38]

While far from conclusive, other research reports also suggest financial wellness training may positively impact stress and related costs the same way employers are finding success in addressing health behaviors. A 2008 study of a public-private partnership found promising results. The partnership combined research from the Federal Reserve Bank of Kansas City with funding from the United Way of the Midlands. The instruction consisted of nine hours of classroom training and up to five one-on-one counseling sessions with a financial planner. The results showed that employee requests for new loans from their 401(k) plans were eliminated, installment debt fell more than 14% and many participants stopped being late on paying their bills. The study did not measure stress directly, but the authors argue there is a link between financial satisfaction and reduced stress:

> Where we did see a significant change in the survey data is in a large increase in the share of participants who felt satisfied with their financial situation two to three years following enrollment. Although we have no way to measure stress directly . . . we expect that increased financial satisfaction leads to reduced stress.[39]

Given the large costs that may be associated with financial stress in terms of productivity loss and higher health care spending, employers have a potentially large incentive to explore cost-effective ways to enhance employee financial wellness. Indeed, employees would also clearly benefit from any programs that reduced stress that may be linked to poor health.

2.3. Employee Engagement

Engaged employees are defined as those who are not only satisfied with their jobs, their companies, and the conditions of their employment, they are also enthusiastic and committed to the mission of the company where they work and they are willing to expend extra effort to see their employer succeed.[40] In seeking to promote engagement, HR professionals are trying to motivate employees "to go the extra mile."[41] While difficult to describe in the abstract, engagement appears to be the difference between satisfying people at work and inspiring them to do their best work.

A common theme in the many surveys of employee engagement is the need for employers to promote a culture that manages employee stress and promotes overall employee wellness. In a 2012 McKinsey/Conference Board survey, two-thirds of the human resources professionals asked considered "health and wellness programs" to be one of the most important actions they could take to promote engagement.[42] And there is some evidence that financially capable employees are more likely to be engaged employees. For example, financial wellness appears to be positively correlated with satisfaction with and pride in the company where one works.[43] Many of the employers and employees contacted for this report volunteered how important their financial wellness programs were to the overall perception of the company and employee motivation. The United Way/Kansas City Federal Reserve program mentioned above also produced higher levels of employee satisfaction with their financial situation. Indeed, employers who participated in the program noted that employees "had more energy" and "higher engagement level at work."[44]

Leveraging Existing Benefits

By adopting and expanding programs that enhance the financial capabilities of their employees, companies can also maximize the leverage they get from existing investments in employee benefits to increase employee satisfaction and engagement. 401(k) plans are a case in point. Employers invest heavily in 401(k) plan design and management, the delivery of investment advice, and matching contributions. The goal is to build employee loyalty for the long run and ensure employees are able to finance their retirement.

Unfortunately, many employees are using their 401(k) plan as an expensive form of emergency savings.[45] Twenty-eight percent of employees have some form of 401(k) loan outstanding.[46]

This creates additional expenses for employers who have to manage the program. For the employees, it is also inefficient to use a long-term savings vehicle to meet short-term needs. Employees who leave their jobs with an outstanding balance also may face tax complications if they cannot immediately repay their loans.

Fortunately, some employers have been able to address this problem. As noted above, after a program combining financial education and one-on-one counseling, employees were less likely to take out 401(k) loans. Employers were also likely to see reduced administrative costs resulting from decreased wage garnishments and an increase in employee take-up of tax-preferred flexible spending accounts.[47]

This example underscores an opportunity that may exist for many employers. Most companies provide financial education to support benefits programs such as a 401(k) plan. The tendency is to make the program the focus, not the employee's specific circumstances. However, more creative and flexible solutions often involve little or no cost, but yield important payoffs. For example, more comprehensive financial education programs that include goal-setting and debt management can provide employees with important context about both the value of their benefits and the importance of balancing short-term needs against long-term goals, whereas training solely on the basics of a 401(k) plan may not. A broader approach to financial skill-building can help employees better understand how a benefits program helps them to manage their financial risks and fits into a comprehensive financial plan.

2.3. Low-Cost/High-Return Opportunity

Employers have invested tremendous resources in wellness programs and health. Programs that build financial capability and enhance financial wellness offer the potential to leverage these investments and create a large payoff for a small expenditure.

The experience of the U.S. Army is a case in point. For some servicemembers, adverse credit reports can cause a security clearance to be suspended or revoked, jeopardizing the ability to perform their jobs. [48] For those serving overseas, financial problems back home may be hard to address and may put unit readiness and morale at risk. Concerned about the impact of financial stress on military personnel, the Department of Defense implemented financial education programs for all the services. To date, hundreds of thousands of servicemembers have been trained in everything from credit management to retirement planning.

A recent study of over 80,000 participants in an Army training program (the Personal Financial Management Course) found positive results with the strongest impact on retirement savings. The average amount contributed to retirement accounts each month roughly doubled, from around $15 per month to over $30. It is worth noting that these contributions were not matched, though they were part of a tax-advantaged saving program, the Thrift Savings Plan (TSP). If those amounts are maintained for just two years, the study's author calculates that this will result in $4,300 in additional savings over a working career.[49]

The Personal Financial Management Course, while only an introductory, eight-hour course, also had a modest, but positive impact on financial decisions about credit cards and auto loans. An examination of 33,000 credit reports showed that course attendees reduced their credit balances (credit cards, auto loans, finance loans, and unpaid balances) by about $635 (10%) and monthly required payments fell by about $37 (17%). But the study found that these effects only persisted as far as one year.[50]

The Army's experience might provide a benchmark for some private sector employers. The eight-hour course has been estimated to cost about $22 per soldier. In the United States, the median hourly wage including benefits is roughly $30, putting a reasonable cost in employee time for an eight-hour training course at roughly $240. But it may also be the case that employees will benefit from an initial comprehensive training followed by shorter, targeted programs. For comparison, one study of corporate wellness programs found that they cost $144 per employee per year on average.[51]

Considering the connection noted earlier between absenteeism and productivity loss and financial stress, the cost of providing a financial wellness program appears manageable for many employers. As an example, a few hours of additional productivity per year or a one-day reduction in absenteeism per participant would likely be enough to cover the employer's per-person training cost. And it is also possible that more effective delivery methods for financial training, including just-in-time guidance, could drive down costs and allow for more rigorous analysis of benefits.

Modest Program Costs

The help employees are seeking need not be expensive or complicated. Financial wellness may simply be a more proactive, cost-effective method of delivering help that employers are already providing. For example, half of the workforce says emergency savings is a major concern.[52] Press accounts and comments from many of the employers and experts contacted for this report tell the same basic story: Employees often approach a manager or human resources officer for a paycheck advance to address an emergency like a car repair that threatens to drain a bank account and make it difficult for that employee to keep his or her job. Employee requests for emergency loans from their employers usually involve fairly modest amounts ranging from enough to cover an auto repair to a few months' rent.

Training programs to help employees build skills in budgeting and saving to address needs before they become emergencies seem like a low-cost opportunity for both employers and employees and would meet a critical employee need. In some instances, informational nudges might be enough to prompt some employees to save for emergencies or other goals. [53] A simple planning aid has been found to improve retirement savings outcomes for employees [54]

Sally Hass, the former Human Resources Director for Weyerhaeuser, argues employers are already "in the financial education business."

Sally Hass, the former Human Resources Director for Weyerhaeuser, argues employers are already "in the financial education business." [55] They provide benefits and educate employees about complicated financial and investment products. However, she says employers rarely "give much thought to the question of how they can be more effective with what they are spending to educate employees." For example, Hass says employers could simply set benchmarks for benefits providers to achieve in providing effective, engaging financial guidance. Another option employers may consider, Hass suggests, is requiring benefits providers to make it easier for employees to find existing resources and use online tools to see how their financial decisions affect their futures.[56] She sees another benefit to these programs - specifically that many industries are facing an exodus of workers with decades of experience who are preparing to walk out the door. As older workers approach retirement, Hass says a strong retirement financial planning program can make a difference by convincing older workers to delay retirement or work part time in order to realistically fund retirement. [57]

2.4. Obstacles to Financial Fitness at Work

While interest in financial wellness appears to be growing, obstacles to wider adoption still remain. Many of the executives contacted for this paper say institutional barriers are a common obstacle. Human resources executives are most likely to interact with employees experiencing financial stress, but the human resource function in many organizations is often not the place where decisions are made about company expenditures to implement a new program. Chief financial officers must usually sign off on new expenditures and they are often less likely to be swayed by the sometimes anecdotal evidence for the benefits of financial wellness programs.

Since human resource functions may be viewed as a cost-center, some employers may also be reluctant to increase expenses, even in cases where a strong benefit is likely. Before committing to launch financial wellness programs, employers say they want customized, proven programs that can be delivered at no additional cost.[58]

The mechanism for delivering financial wellness programs may be as important as the content. Employees may be reluctant to discuss embarrassing financial information with coworkers or even with contractors hired by an employer to deliver financial education unless it becomes more of an ingrained part of the workplace culture. Making financial wellness training a more regular benefit offering or activity may help overcome the perception that this is an emergency service or a form of remedial training.

There are also some philosophical and other obstacles to financial wellness programs. Employers may not feel it is appropriate or desirable for them to advise their employees on financial management. There is concern financial wellness programs may intrude on employee privacy or put employers in the uncomfortable position of making value judgments about employee spending preferences. Some employers are also wary of legal liability if they endorse or partner with programs that offer financial education.[59]

But even with those concerns, the employers mentioned in this report have found a way to balance the desire to assist employees with the need to respect employees' privacy and personal financial decisions. Employers have also found ways to provide financial wellness programs without unduly raising the possibility of legal liability.

Limited Initial Research Findings

Another significant barrier to financial wellness programs is the limited amount of reliable research on effectiveness, cost-savings, and productivity impacts from such programs.[60] Many studies rely on self-assessments and the underlying programs reflect the self-selection bias of participants.[61] Employers that implement financial wellness training programs may also typically have employee characteristics that make those programs more likely to succeed.[62]

Measuring the direct monetary benefit from workplace financial education is also not easy. The financial information employees receive is most often provided in the context of a discussion of retirement benefits and is delivered by a financial provider or consultant. A much smaller subset of employers offer basic assistance with budgeting, emergency savings, planning for college and other important events. Even that type of assistance is not usually delivered in the context that some experts in the field argue will be most effective. Some researchers have suggested that delivering financial education or counseling close in time to a decision point – a strategy sometimes called "just-in-time" – may be most effective.[63] On top of all this, it is inherently difficult to link any single program to a bottom line impact that might reduce costs and enhance profitability. Finally, an employee's overall financial wellness is a complex interaction between variables employers can influence through training programs – such as an employee's financial skills – and external factors that are harder to gauge and influence – such as an employees' perception of broader macro-economic trends.

That said, it is critical to try to better understand the impact of financial wellness programs on the issues about which employers care most about: engagement, absenteeism, stress, and health-related costs. The opportunity exists for health researchers to partner with non-profits and companies providing financial capability training to craft studies that measure financial and overall stress levels before and after receiving budgeting, debt management, and other financial wellness interventions. Further, the connections between long-term financial stress and health outcomes can be studied more closely.

It would also be useful to better understand the benefits of differentiating financial wellness approaches for different employee groups. For example, some studies find that programs that are highly-targeted to a specific demographic group or financial activity are most effective or that low-income workers need the most help in managing money and benefit the most from financial education.[64] There may also be interesting research around how different financial wellness approaches vary in effectiveness at different stages of the employee lifecycle; it stands to reason that new employees might most benefit from a different set of trainings or skill building exercises than employees approaching retirement. And there is also much work to do in studying the effectiveness of new, lower-cost interventions tied to online and mobile applications.

While there is still much to be learned, many employers are taking the approach of building on what does work and learning by doing, understanding that the lack of perfect information need not prevent reasonable steps that can be taken now. Some of those steps will be examined in the next section.

3. Promising Practices in Workplace Financial Wellness

Employers are deeply aware of the financial stress most Americans struggle with every day. Many companies are moved to help employees navigate their financial troubles because they consider it "the right thing to do." But employers who are motivated to take the next step and develop comprehensive financial wellness programs do so for different reasons. Some have a tradition of supporting employees that developed from the philosophy of a founder or influential leader early in the organization's history. Others have been moved to act by the struggles of an individual employee or by an executive's personal interest in financial education.

In addition to personal and philosophical reasons for taking on this challenge, many businesses believe financial wellness programs generate greater engagement, loyalty and productivity. These are some of the themes that emerged from discussions with employers:

- Employers are keenly aware of the financial stress facing many employees and they are genuinely interested in helping the people who work for them.
- Customer-centric businesses are worried that financially stressed employees will not provide the level of service required to succeed in a competitive marketplace.
- Human resources professionals are concerned matching funds in 401(k) programs are being used to meet short-term emergencies, undermining an expensive benefit program.

- Many employers believe financial wellness programs are an important way for employers to show they genuinely care about employees and are an effective way to reduce employee turnover and build loyalty.[65]

The examples of workplace financial education in action that follow are not intended to be representative of all the work being done in this area. Rather, the intention is to present a range of experience from some leading employers in the country that might be helpful to others who are considering steps to promote financial wellness and address financial stress in the workplace.

3.1. The Power of Peer-to-Peer Support

Andrew Rosenkranz became interested in providing financial counseling and money management training for his employees because he was running out of answers. Like many business owners, Rosenkranz found his employees at Pacific Research[66] often turned to him for advice.

While the company has provided support and advice to employees on a case-by-case basis, it has limited resources, and is unable to do so comprehensively, or to provide the level of support needed to effectively solve more complex financial issues. In some cases, workers have asked about high-cost loans and other expensive financial products. Rosenkranz noted that many Pacific Research employees had only a limited financial education and little access to professional advice. They often turn to friends who may have little more experience with financial decisions.

As challenges grew, Rosenkranz turned to a program run by Neighborhood Trust Financial Partners to help employers offer financial skills training and counseling to employees. The training included individual counseling and classroom instruction in budget basics as well as other financial skills such as setting up direct deposit and dealing with debt collectors.[67]

Rosenkranz says: “A lot of these people are so overwhelmed and are in such a bad financial strait that they don’t know where to start so they ignore the problem. The most effective part of the program was real-time help. For example, a counselor with the program might meet with an employee and walk them through a credit report and then offer to call about a bill while the employee listens in and learns to negotiate a reasonable payment plan.”

Rosenkranz found some of the most important and lasting outcomes from the program came from positive peer pressure at work. Employees formed teams of two or three or four people encouraging each other and trying to hold each other to solid financial principals.[68] Work teams that went through training together made financial planning almost into a game.

Fostering these kinds of peer-to-peer interactions is an important part of Neighborhood Trust's training strategy. Neighborhood Trust points to research that suggests coworkers can help each other develop better financial habits. The training programs at Pacific Research were designed to encourage peer-to-peer interactions "by creating a 'safe' environment where participants feel they can share their questions and experience without being judged."[69] Participants in the trainings were encouraged to discuss their experiences with the people seated around them. The end goal is a supportive, collaborative environment.[70]

Neighborhood Trust reports virtually all the participants in the Pacific Research program said they would recommend it to a friend or co-worker, with eight out of ten saying they would do so "strongly." The same number report (78%) they have made a positive change in their spending habits as a result of the training. For Pacific Research, the training has resulted in a boost to employee perceptions, increasing from 48% to 81% the percentage who see their employer as caring about their well-being.

Most of the employers contacted for this report shared similar stories. Some said both managers and employees found discussions with peers and support from co-workers provided powerful motivation to adopt positive financial behaviors. While lower paid workers had more difficulty making ends meet, even managers and more highly compensated employees reported challenges tracking spending and balancing immediate needs against longer-term priorities. One employee survey found that 17% of employees making more than $100,000 relied on credit cards for "monthly necessities."[71]

These are the people you work with every day and you want to equip them with skills that will improve their lives.

While there are likely benefits to employers who provide financial capabilities training to employees in terms of increased loyalty and reduced absenteeism, a key benefit for many small business owners may be personal. As Rosenkranz points out, the people he helped support are his co-workers and peers: "These are the people you work with every day and you want to equip them with skills that will improve their lives."

3.2. Leveraging Technology to Lower Costs and Deliver Scale

As a global company with operations in 25 countries and 1,800 stores in North America, Staples does not have a one-size-fits-all workforce. It may have hundreds of people working at a warehouse or call center, but only a few dozen at a local retail store. Human resources executives at Staples understood any financial wellness program they chose would have to be adaptable enough to be delivered effectively in different work settings and in a way that fit with busy schedules. A financial skills-building course that might be cost-effective at a large facility could be very impractical at a small store. Staples also realized any financial wellness program it adopted would have to be scalable to serve a global company.

Gamification

Staples realized it needed to start thinking more broadly about financial health of its associates when it came time to sign employees up for the company 401(k). At first, Staples thought it had a communication problem. Participation rates were disappointing. Executives thought workers didn't understand the benefits – that employees didn't realize they were giving up free money by passing on the company match. Or that the low participation rate might indicate a structural problem. Perhaps the program was too difficult to navigate or the barriers to participation were too high? Staples started experimenting with simplifying enrollment and changing eligibility requirements.

To learn more, Lisa Blasdale, Staples Senior Benefits Manager, made a special effort to get out into the field, touring facilities and meeting associates. Initially, Blasdale says employees would not talk to her about why they were not participating in the 401(k) plan. But after people got to know and trust her, associates began to share their stories. Blasdale learned many long-time Staples associates did not believe they had enough money to save anything. They reported that they were struggling with debt or basic credit issues. The conversations, she says, were "eye opening."

Blasdale realized Staples needed a new approach to increase engagement and help associates. The company decided to refocus its efforts on basic financial management skills. The new programs emphasized the need to manage spending and make room to pay down high-interest debt. Staples also worked harder to explain the benefits of saving for retirement.

But the critical challenge was not just helping associates learn to manage their money, the problem was finding a way to develop programs that could deliver highly engaging financial wellness training at scale for a diverse, far-flung workforce. Blasdale was concerned a typical classroom training on financial skills would be impractical and expensive to implement and it would be too boring to engage associates. Staples wanted an easier approach and got it. Through a connection at Progress Through Business, a nonprofit group supporting entrepreneurship and financial literacy, Staples was introduced to a nonprofit game designer applying financial innovation and entertainment to support the economic success of low-to-moderate income families. Bite Club, an online game Staples decided to use, offers players a chance to manage a nightclub for vampires. As they play, employees must decide between priorities like investing in a 401(k), paying off student debt, and buying some "bling."[72] The goal is to link game play to positive action that benefits the employee.

The game also tapped into the positive power of peer-to-peer interactions by encouraging associates in Staples stores and regions to compete against each other. The contests appeal to the competitive nature of many associates, while fostering collaboration by encouraging employees within a store or region to support each other as they work to improve their financial health. In two different districts, Staples noted that roughly 80% of targeted employees engaged with the company's game portal page. [73]

It is really a business imperative if you really want to be competitive right now. You really have to have a productive workforce and in order to have a productive workforce they need to feel great about themselves.

For Staples, financial wellness has become a critical factor in engaging employees. Blasdale says: "It is really a business imperative if you really want to be competitive right now. You really have to have a productive workforce and in order to have a productive workforce they need to feel great about themselves. They shouldn't have to worry about how many bill collectors will contact them after they leave the place of employment."

Bite Club was developed by the nonprofit, Doorways2Dreams, and encouraged by the reception to Bite Club, Staples is rolling out new games from the same source. Farm Blitz will encourage associates to build emergency savings as they manage farm resources. Refund Rush helps people learn to "split" their tax refunds, dividing their deposits into savings and checking accounts. Blasdale says, "Right now, we might not be able to get them to increase their 401(k) contribution, but that's fine as long as they are not acquiring more debt."

Staples' experience has helped convince plan providers to offer games to other companies as a way to boost 401(k) participation and encourage financial wellness.

3.3. Case Studies in Promoting Financial Wellness: the Promise of Public-Private Partnerships

In 2004, the Federal Reserve Bank of Kansas City and Omaha-based United Way of the Midlands (UWM) joined forces to address rising signs of financial stress in the workforce. Staff at the two institutions decided to implement a program based on a wellness model that was designed to be similar to "working with a physical fitness trainer." Employees in the area would be offered a personal finance course and access to one-on-one counseling sessions with a certified financial planner. The program would be delivered in the workplace and researchers at the Federal Reserve Bank of Kansas City would study the results.

After an initial pilot, United Way of the Midlands raised $10,000 to launch three test sites in Omaha, Nebraska. Classes began in May 2006. Perhaps the most impressive result is that employers who participated in the pilot program still offer it today.

Public-private partnerships like this have been an effective way to raise awareness of the challenges of financial stress in the workplace and have encouraged employers to test drive financial wellness programs across the country. The participation of respected non-profits helps companies overcome concerns about the potential risk of offering basic financial advice to employees. And public-sector institutions often bring important research skills needed to validate the effectiveness of financial wellness interventions.

Emotions and Money

Waddell & Reed, the asset management company selected to provide the training to participants in the Omaha area, developed an unconventional approach to financial wellness training. Shawn Macken, a financial advisor at Waddell & Reed has spent more than a decade delivering financial education and wellness program instruction to employees in the Omaha area. When he first began offering traditional "lunch and learns," Macken covered traditional topics such as retirement planning and college funding. But he quickly saw that the "tried and true" approach did not seem to be very effective. Macken began searching for more effective methods to deal with the underlying issues that he believed motivated financial behaviors. Macken says he came to see that "if you ignore emotion in this process, you are going to miss the point."

After one of his presentations, a client suggested Macken's approach was similar to the model used by the Omaha-based Wellness Council of the Midlands. As a result of the client's introduction, Macken adapted the principles of the wellness model – awareness, education and behavior change. It is the last part of the process – behavior change – that, according to Macken, brings emotions about money into play.

In the Omaha public-private partnership, employees attended a nine-week classroom course plus and received one year of one-on-one comprehensive financial planning services. The classroom sessions included courses on traditional money management topics such as budgeting and credit, but the sessions also addressed the fears that often motivate or underlie poor financial decisions. As the classroom sessions and financial planning meetings progressed, the instructor and the financial advisor reassured participants that the mistakes they make and the feelings they have about money are normal and to be expected.

The training delivered through the Omaha program reassures employees that their financial mistakes are a result of very human traits. For example, employees who are in debt may try to pay off what they owe too quickly, leaving little money for emergencies. Macken argues this cycle is driven in large part by fear of debt. If employees are to successfully work their way out of debt, Macken argues, "Emotionally, you have to break that feast and famine cycle."

The next step was to discuss actions employees could take to increase their chances of being financially successful. Spouses were encouraged to attend these one-on-one sessions as well. If employees have trust in the planners, Macken argues they are open to adopting a financial plan that accounts for emotions and weaknesses in human decision-making. The focus on emotions may seem odd to some given the dry reputation of most financial planning programs, but it is a theme that comes up again and again in successful programs.

Below are case studies from two employers who participated in the initial Omaha program and still offer it.

QLI: Keeping Turnover Down and Retaining a Dedicated Staff

QLI's mission is to serve adults who have suffered a catastrophic injury. It is demanding work that requires a dedicated staff and a long-term commitment. Early on this realization informed QLI's strategy to invest in retaining employees in an industry renowned for high turnover.

To succeed in the demanding work of caring for people with disabilities, QLI CEO Patricia Kearns argues employees need to develop what she calls the "emotional resilience" to cope with the needs of patients and families in crisis. But Kearns realized several years ago many of her own employees were in crisis. Staff members were asking for advances on their paychecks. Conversations with employees showed some were living beyond their means. Few young staff members were knowledgeable about saving for retirement. A shockingly low number were saving through QLI's retirement plan.

"Financial stressors are one of the bigger things that all our staff struggle with in their personal life," says QLI CEO Patricia Kearns. QLI leadership decided it was time to act. Mary Sheldrick is one of the employees QLI invested in keeping. Sheldrick had run into financial problems making ends meet on the wages typically paid to health care workers in this field. She says her self-esteem plummeted as her financial situation began to spiral down: "When you are in this kind of situation, your self-esteem is affected if you have bill collectors calling you and making you feel like crap if you can't pay them."

Sheldrick was an eager participant in the financial training program offered through the partnership with the Kansas City Federal Reserve Bank, UWM, and Waddell & Reed. Two things struck her about the program. First, the training offered practical, step-by-step methods to address common financial problems. The training materials showed Sheldrick and others how to examine their debt and manage their pocketbooks more effectively. Perhaps most importantly, the training also addressed the emotional concerns that arise when people fall into debt and other financial trouble.

Sheldrick explains, "What they did is they helped us see that all of us in the class were good people and smart people, and we had to get past the shame that everybody in this class has debt and made mistakes." The explicit recognition of employee feelings around their financial situation appears to be an important factor in the program's success.

QLI executives participated in the training to vet the curriculum. And they also came away learning valuable financial skills and methods to better manage their spending. QLI's director of human resources agreed the emotional context of the program was an important aspect of its success.

The experience of building financial skills with co-workers also created a sense of camaraderie. As we have seen with other programs, peer-to-peer interaction helped QLI employees struggling with financial issues. Sheldrick explains: "You feel a sense of humility in a force of many where you have one cause and are working together on it."

To QLI leadership the business case for financial training is clear. Employees are coming to work and are able to focus and give exceptional customer service "rather than worrying which bill collector will call and making mistakes on the job because they aren't paying attention."[74] In a health care context, employee focus is particularly critical. Alicia Elson, QLI's Vice President of Human Resources, says, "That $300 we paid for the financial education class is a lot cheaper than that potential malpractice lawsuit we might have (if an employee is distracted at work)."

Patricia Kearns, QLI's CEO, says financial wellness training "is one of the most important things we do."

Patricia Kearns, QLI's CEO, says financial wellness training "is one of the most important things we do." It is one reason the company's turnover rate for employees it wants to keep hovers between six and nine percent[75] – a rate much lower than the high turnover rate that is common in the rehabilitation industry.[76] QLI finds a lower turnover rate helps keep costs and staffing needs in human resources down as well. Also, the company doesn't have to pay as much overtime, because it is able to retain employees and keep a dependable schedule without the disruptions that come with high staff turnover.

QLI is now in the eighth year of offering the financial wellness program and 70% of the staff has participated. The company's management believes the financial training succeeded in large part because of the combination of a well-thought out structure involving skilled trainers, sophisticated materials, rigorous research, and a committed employer. The training was reinforced in the workplace by bringing co-workers together to support each other. QLI employees are encouraged to pay a portion of the program's cost to encourage buy-in. The financial wellness training continues to be highly valued by employees and is seen as a benefit that can distinguish employers who compete to be considered "best companies to work for."

Nebraska Furniture Mart

Rose Blumkin, better known as "Mrs. B," the legendary founder of Nebraska Furniture Mart (NFM), lived by the motto "sell cheap and tell the truth." And true to that philosophy, when Mrs.'s B's grandson Ron Blumkin, the President of NFM, found out the Kansas City Federal Reserve Bank was putting together a free program for employers to offer financial education to their workers, he liked the price and signed the company up.

After I got a plan, my finances did not change. But, for first time in my life, I thought there was a light at the end of the tunnel, and I realized the birds were chirping.

The first classes at NFM, which became a subsidiary of Berkshire Hathaway in 1983, enrolled twenty employees. An NFM human resources executive still remembers the comments she heard at the final session. An employee who had taken numerous loans from her 401(k) said, “After I got a plan, my finances did not change. But, for first time in my life, I thought there was a light at the end of the tunnel, and I realized the birds were chirping.”

Other stories were less dramatic, but spoke to the deep impact the program had on NFM employees. One employee said she thought at the time she would be able to pay for all of their children’s college. But after taking the program, she realized that she realistically could save for half. Another employee said he was talking with friends after work and recalled how one said, “Wow, I can’t believe your company is offering something like that.” Both moved and concerned by these stories, NFM executives decided to keep offering the financial wellness program and to expand it.

NFM says that two hundred employees have completed the financial wellness program so far. The company credits the training with reducing 401(k) loans among this population. In addition, the program has been particularly effective in helping employees who work on commission. Since these workers have paychecks that fluctuate, financial training was effective in coming up with ways to better plan for swings in income by transferring a set amount of money to a checking account every month. Counselors also helped employees to set up automatic transfers to implement the cash flow management.

NFM finds the financial wellness training is a good way to reinforce values that matter to the company. The courses helped employees to understand and put a financial value on their health insurance and what it really costs. The company also has a very strict policy on 401(k) loans. Executives believe the program is not designed for short-term savings. The financial training courses reinforce this corporate message and help NFM counter a common issue raised by new employees: “My old employer let me take a loan out for any reason.” NFM executives say it is helpful to have a third party back up company values.

With a long-term orientation consistent with other Berkshire Hathaway companies, NFM aims to make a lasting connection with customers and employees. Its turnover rate is just 20%, a low figure for the retail industry. NFM believes that employees recognize the company is doing something special for them by offering financial wellness training because it cares about their well-being and that has helped reduce turnover.

As Megan Berry Barlow, Human Resources Director for NFM, puts it, "Helping somebody save for retirement doesn't make them rich today, so if you are not taking a long-term path to help someone stay here for 10 to 15 years, a program like this might not make much sense if you didn't have a long term orientation."

NFM also views financial wellness as a gap in society that employers can fill. Rather than pass the buck to someone else, NFM wants to do its share to help employees plan for retirement and to meet other important life goals.[77] The private-public partnership with the Federal Reserve Bank of Kansas City and the United Way of the Midlands helped catalyze NFM's ability to act to support its employees in a fundamental way.

Public-Private Partnerships at Scale: Delaware's $t and by Me®

In several places in this report we have discussed the power of public-private partnerships to support employers and help them to take action. In Delaware, a public private partnership has gone a step further, seeding the development of financial wellness programs across the state and in a wide range of sectors. Delaware's experience demonstrates financial wellness programs can be delivered by employers in many different sectors and at scale.

Working with the United Way of Delaware and private foundations including the Delaware Community Foundation and the Kellogg Foundation, Delaware's Governor Jack Markell and the state of Delaware supports the delivery of financial coaching services through a joint venture called "$tand By Me." Since 2011, more than 8,000 financial coaching sessions have been held at community colleges, state agencies and workplaces across the state. $tand by Me now serves some 1,200 employees at fifty different employers.

$tand by Me focuses on employers in sectors that traditionally hire lower-wage workers. Financial coaches are currently working at over 40 child care and Head Start centers. Most of the major hospitals in the state have signed on to the $tand by Me effort. For example, Christiana Health Systems, the state's largest health care provider, is paying for a coach to offer financial coaching as a benefit available to its 10,000 employees. The joint venture has reached a broad range of employers, including a major state agency, a supermarket chain and two large hotels. All of the coaches are employed by independent non-profit organizations, who are contracted, trained, and managed by $tand By Me. This separation from the employer's HR department is seen by $tand by Me as critical as it supports the employees' need for complete confidentiality in their relationship with the coach, as they tackle their personal financial challenges.

Mary DuPont, Delaware's Director of Financial Empowerment, says, "When employers experience the benefit it brings to their workforce, it becomes part of their culture and then external support is no longer needed."

To engage with employees, $tand by Me also offers an incentive program modelled on those offered by traditional wellness programs. Employees who participate in the *FinFit* program can earn points for taking financially "healthy" behaviors. For example, employees who attend a workshop earn 25 points. A financial coaching session earns 50 points. An employee who sets up a budget earns 25 points. At 200 points, an employee is eligible for a $25 gift card. Earn another 100 points and an employee can win a $50 certificate of deposit.

A key goal of the partnership is to demonstrate for employers the value of providing financial wellness programs. Mary DuPont, Delaware's Director of Financial Empowerment, says, "When employers experience the benefit it brings to their workforce, it becomes part of their culture and then external support is no longer needed."

3.4. Financial Fitness Starting at Employee Onboarding

In 2012, working through its network of community-based agencies across the United States and Canada, Goodwill Industries International provided employment and training programs to almost seven million people, many of whom have disabilities, criminal backgrounds, or other challenges that make it difficult to find employment. In addition to these challenges, the people Goodwill serves may not have had much experience or success managing their money. The combination of these challenges convinced Goodwill Central Texas (GCT) to integrate financial wellness into its employee training with the goal of increasing the long-term work success for people who face so many employment challenges.

Steve Stokes, Financial Wellness Coordinator for Goodwill Central Texas, says, "We needed to do things to get ahead of the problem rather than trying to chase it and put out fires."

Full-time, entry-level employees at GCT earn an average of $17,160 a year. Goodwill managers have seen how their employees may be vulnerable to high-cost credit or may have difficulty building up their credit scores. Steve Stokes, Financial Wellness Coordinator for Goodwill Central Texas, says, "We needed to do things to get ahead of the problem rather than trying to chase it and put out fires."

Working with Nancy Klein, GCT's Employee Assistance Program Coordinator, Stokes developed a comprehensive financial wellness program and decided to deliver it during the onboarding process for new employees. Onboarding was selected as the delivery point, because GCT considers it to be a "milestone moment" when employees are open to change. Stokes defines milestones such as the start of a new job as moments when "something major is happening" which creates an "opportunity for [employees] to consider alternative ways to do things, especially if how they were doing them in the past was not working for them."[78]

By taking advantage of the new employee orientation, 15 to 20 new hires a week are offered at least three opportunities to improve their financial wellness. First, all new hires complete a Financial Wellness ssessment and participate in a one-hour workshop called *Financial Recovery!* In the classroom setting, employees cover goal-setting, budgeting, and the cost of credit. The curriculum is based on the FDIC's MoneySmart Program. Second, employees are offered the opportunity to participate in one-on-one financial counseling provided through the EAP program. Third, employees can sign up for financial coaching.

Like many organizations, GCT considers coaching and counseling to be distinct programs. Financial counseling is crisis-driven and counselors focus on resolving problems in a confidential setting. After an initial assessment counselors will develop a service plan to address a new employee's individual needs. Financial needs will often surface as a factor for employees who seek EAP counseling for stress, substance abuse, or other problems. In those cases a Financial Wellness Counselor will assist the EAP Counselor in counseling an employee.

In contrast, financial coaching is aimed not at crisis resolution, but at helping employees achieve goals they define themselves. Financial coaches work with new GCT hires to help them set and achieve goals such as putting together a spending plan or a savings plan to meet other priorities. Individual coaching sessions offer a chance to probe and ask important questions aimed at improving “long term financial behavior.” For example, Stokes says a coach might ask, “If you have been budgeting in your head instead of on paper, how is that working for you?” Stokes adds, “We try to give [employees] an alternative way to think about this.” The process is client-driven with behavior change to support improved outcomes desired by the consumer as an end-goal.

GCT has also found onboarding is a natural time to introduce employees to University Federal Credit Union, a Goodwill Community Partner. Because GCT requires direct deposit, employees without a bank account are given the opportunity to choose between a UFCU checking account, a savings account with an ATM card or a payroll card.

While the financial wellness program was designed with low-income workers in mind, GCT has also found onboarding training is helping managers as well. Managers save time and have less stress when they know an employee is getting the help they need to address a stressful financial problem. Employees who may be facing eviction or are in danger of losing their car are less likely to be successful in completing training sessions or focusing on work. GCT’s financial training is also directly helping its professional staff – including some who are professionals with college degrees. Trainers say incomes may differ, but many people lack basic financial knowledge regardless of their education level.

At 60 days and again in annual trainings GCT marks additional milestone moments. After 60 days, the financial wellness concepts introduced at onboarding are reinforced by requiring GCT employees to attend another full-day of benefits training which includes a financial education segment. Stokes explains that many GCT employees are marketed high-cost payday, used car, and car title loans. The 60-day training covers the wise use of credit and informs workers of alternatives to expensive credit products. Financial wellness messages are also reinforced for longer-term employees at mandatory annual training sessions which cover the need to think about longer-term milestones including savings and preparation for retirement.

In addition, GCT has developed an Emergency Employee Advance Program to help meet unexpected, emergency expenses. Eligible employees who apply for an advance must attend a financial counseling session and are limited to one advance per year. After documenting the need for the advance, employees are allowed to direct the payment of up to the net amount, excluding overtime, of one paycheck to a business where they have an unexpected or overdue bill. There are no fees, no interest is charged, and the advance is paid back through deductions from regular bi-weekly paychecks. The goal is to help employees who may not be able to get a traditional loan to reduce their reliance on payday lenders. [79]

GCT is not alone in recognizing the opportunity to introduce better financial skills at onboarding. Staples is now working to integrate financial wellness opportunities into the onboarding process. These employers see the onboarding process as an opportune time to introduce financial training. At onboarding, new employees are focused on making important financial decisions such as choices about withholding, retirement savings, and employer-offered health insurance.

4. Takeaways, Next Steps for Consideration, and CFPB Resources

Many Americans find money to be an endless source of stress. Too many workers are one car repair away from losing their ability to get to work and earn a living. Even a basic emergency can throw a family into a spiral of debt. Despite the many benefits employers provide to their workers, employees are asking for something that is fairly basic and that will most likely not cost that much to provide: help. Help managing their money. Help planning and budgeting to make ends meet. Help setting aside a small amount for the next emergency they know is coming. Fortunately, it appears employers may be able to provide their employee's with the help they seek while helping their own bottom lines.

The promising practices outlined in this report demonstrate that employers can increase their employees' engagement and productivity and help their workers achieve financial peace of mind. These practices include:

- Listening to employees and establishing trust. Employers report the value of a concerted effort to talk with and survey employees about their financial needs before crafting a financial wellness plan. HR professionals stress that employees are unlikely to respond to a financial wellness program if they do not feel the company has listened to them and can be trusted to act in their best interests. Some employers have hired outside companies to provide financial coaching and education, in part to reassure employees that the programs will be confidential.

- Tapping peer-to-peer support. Research and employer experience confirm that employees learn important financial lessons from each other. Financial wellness programs are more likely to succeed when employees support each other in developing positive financial habits.
- Leveraging technology to lower costs and deliver scale. Employers report that financial games and mobile tools hold great promise to deliver engaging, affordable financial wellness programs at scale.
- Forging or tapping into public-private partnerships. The United Way of the Midlands, the Federal Reserve Bank of Kansas City and private employers came together to develop and deliver a successful and ongoing financial wellness program for modest expense. Local foundations, government agencies, civic organizations, and business groups have served as catalysts for public-private partnerships across the country.
- Presenting financial wellness at onboarding. Goodwill Central Texas and other employers are implementing financial wellness at onboarding seeing it as a natural complement to new employee orientation and the benefits selection process.

The employers and experts contacted for this report also shared the following general observations about the effectiveness of financial wellness programs and the usefulness of exploring the connection between financial stress and health care costs.

- **Successful financial wellness programs are cost-effective.** Program delivery need not be expensive or burdensome. Public-private partnerships have successfully tested program features and reduced delivery costs. New mobile financial management applications and innovative tools such as financial games also hold great promise in reducing cost and reaching scale.
- **Employers say employees highly value effective financial wellness programs delivered in the context of a trusting work environment.** Employers who accepted where their employees were financially and responded with programs to meet pressing employee needs in a trusting, non-judgmental manner reported increased employee engagement, fewer days lost to absenteeism, and lower administrative costs associated with 401(k) loans and wage garnishments.

- **Some financial wellness programs support the development of more successful financial habits by addressing emotional factors that may contribute to poor financial decision-making.** For example, the financial coaches interviewed for this report say programs that are designed to help employees resolve feelings of fear or embarrassment over their financial situation are more likely to prompt employees to act to develop more positive financial habits.
- **Employers would find it helpful to better quantify how financial wellness programs benefit employees and employers.** More needs to be done to highlight and measure which approaches are most successful in reducing stress and producing lasting positive changes for employees in terms of health and financial outcomes.

Next Steps: Additional Program Elements Employers May want to Consider

While employers evaluate the specific needs of their employees and formulate an appropriate response, there are also initial steps they can take to help set workers on the path to a more secure financial future. Some of these are steps that many employers, including those mentioned in this report, are adopting or considering as they ramp up their own workplace financial wellness programs.

- **Promote split allocation of income to savings and investing**. The use of direct deposit is mandated for all federal employees, and many private sector companies are already encouraging their employees to use direct deposit for their paycheck. Employers in both the public and private sector have the opportunity to use the time of sign up for direct deposit to encourage employees to split their paycheck and automatically save a portion of their pay in a savings vehicle such as an emergency savings account, a brokerage account, an IRA, or a 529 education plan.
- **Support automatic contribution escalation (ACE) to retirement accounts**. The Pension Protection Act of 2006 (PPA) created incentives for plan sponsors to implement automatic enrollment with its 401(k) safe-harbor auto-enrollment and auto-escalation provisions which automatically increase employee contribution rates over time. In some cases, this simple step raises average participation rates from 67% to over 85%.[80]

- **Financial education tied to major life changes and critical needs.** Employers and experts contacted for this report suggested it would be particularly valuable to provide employees with financial education tied to major life changes and critical needs. For example:
  - Saving for emergencies;
  - Managing debt and using credit wisely. For many employees managing debt and credit wisely has a direct impact on their job. While general education on the topic of debt and using credit wisely will be beneficial to all employees, more specific topics such as student loan debt or underwater mortgages might also be appropriate;
  - Budgeting (spending plan development) Young families, for example, may be more receptive to information about saving for college or buying a new home if it is timed to be delivered before or after the birth of a child;
  - Financial goal setting and decision making including help planning for major purchases. Employers could offer education for employees looking to purchase specific assets or to plan for purchasing specific assets such as a home, a car, or a higher education.

The CFPB intends to assist employers as they search for cost-effective solutions to reduce employee financial stress. In particular, the next session details some of the tools the Bureau has developed which employers could use in their workplace financial wellness efforts.

4.1. The CFPB Strategy to Support Financial Wellness

The Dodd-Frank Wall Street Reform and Consumer Protection Act authorizes the CFPB to develop and implement initiatives intended to educate and empower consumers to make better informed financial decisions. To achieve that mission, the CFPB believes it is important to support the delivery of effective financial education in the workplace. After all, the workplace is where most Americans make critical decisions about how to allocate their wages to current needs, savings, investing and important life goals.

This report is one way the Bureau intends to support financial wellness programs at work. Employers who are interested in supporting the financial well-being of their employees may find it valuable to understand the best research about the field, and, perhaps more importantly, a better understanding of what other employers have found works for them. The CFPB can help address this need by bringing together and disseminating information about promising practices in the field.

The CFPB also supports financial wellness at work through the development of tools that help consumers understand important issues and plan for important goals. For example, our online tool, Ask CFPB provides accurate, authoritative, and understandable answers to more than 1,000 common consumer questions about consumer financial products and services (http://www.consumerfinance.gov/askcfpb/). Since its launch, more than two million consumers have used Ask CFPB and it is the CFPB's hope and intention that this database will prove useful to employers who wish to provide their employees with a resource for accurate information about financial products and choices.

The CFPB has also developed the Paying for College tool for students and their families trying to compare financial aid packages from different schools or assess their options for repaying their student debt. Paying for College (http://www.consumerfinance.gov/paying-for-college/) starts with school choice, and goes right through paying those loans back after graduation. Students who use the tool will get guidance in the questions that they should ask and answers they should seek in the college funding decision. They will also build life skills in areas such as planning ahead, identifying key questions and getting answers and comparison shopping– that will help them as consumers throughout their lives.

The CFPB also recognizes that the field of financial education in general would benefit from more foundational research and broader dissemination of techniques and approaches that are supported by reliable research. The CFPB is already conducting research in the field of financial education and will be active in coming years in working with employers to understand how these findings can be applied in the workplace.

Employers are already offering the most essential element to securing financial well-being: a job. The CFPB recognizes the critical role employers play and is encouraged that so many are willing and eager to take the initiative of going even further to support employees in developing the financial skills needed to reduce stress and achieve lasting success for individuals and families across the country.

End Notes

[1] CFPB, Financial Literacy Annual Report 3 (July 2014), available at http://files.consumerfinance.gov/f/201407_cfpb_report_financial-literacy-annual-report.pdf.

[2] American Dream and Financial Security, Washington Post-Miller Center Poll (Sept. 6-12), Washington Post, http://www.washingtonpost.com/politics/polling/postmiller-center-poll-american-dream-financial/2013/11/25/b9cec6ca-2892-11e3-8ab3-b5aacc9e1165_page.html ; see also, e.g., Rakesh Kochhar & Rich Morin, Despite recovery, fewer Americans identify as middle class, Pew Research Center (Jan. 27, 2014), http://www.pewresearch.org/fact-tank/2014/01/27/despite-recovery-fewer-americans-identify-as-middle-class/.

[3] Share of U.S. Workers Living Paycheck to Paycheck Continues to Decline from Recession-Era Peak, Finds Annual CareerBuilder Survey, CareerBuilder, LLC (Sept. 25, 2013), http://www.careerbuilder.com/share/aboutus/pressreleasesdetail.aspx?sd=9%2F25%2F2013 &id=pr781&ed=12%2F31%2F2013 (finding in a survey by Harris Interactive Poll that 36% of those surveyed report they "always or usually live paycheck to paycheck. Posing the question somewhat differently, the American Payroll Association, using a larger survey of more than 30,000, found 68% said they would find it "somewhat or very difficult" if their paychecks were delayed for a week).

[4] Frank Newport, Americans See Finances as Better, but Worse Than Pre-2008, Gallup Economy (Apr. 25, 2013), http://www.gallup.com/poll/162056/americans-finances-better-worse-pre-2008.aspx (The poll finds 40% of respondents say their personal financial situation is "only fair" and 14% see it as "poor," but 47% see it as getting better).

[5] American Psychology Association, Stress in America: Are Teens Adopting Adults' Stress Habits? (2014), available at http://www.apa.org/news/press/releases/stress/2013/stress-report.pdf; PricewaterhouseCoopers, LLC, Employee Financial Wellness Survey 10 (2014), available at http://www.pwc.com/en_US/us/private-company-services pwc- employee-financial-wellness-survey-2014-results.pdf.

[6] FINRA Investor Education Foundation, Financial Capability Study: U.S., http://www.usfinancialcapability.org/results.php?region=US (last visited Aug. 21, 2014).

[7] Id.

[8] See E. Thomas Garman et al., Financial Stress Among American Workers: Final report: 30 Million Workers in America—One in Four—Are Seriously Financially Distressed and Dissatisfied Causing Negative Impacts on Individuals, Families, and Employers 17 (2005), http://www.personalfinancefoundation.org/features/feature-3full.pdf.

[9] Aon Hewitt, 2014 Hot Topics in Retirement 2 (2014), available at http://www.aon.com/attachments/human-capital-consulting/2014_Hot-Topics-Retirement_Report_vFinal(1).pdf

[10] *Id.* at 3.

[11] See, e.g., *AICPA Survey: Money Stress Taking Toll on Well-being*, American Institute of CPAs (Apr. 23, 2013), http://www.aicpa.org/press/pressreleases/2013/pages/aicpa-survey-money-stress-taking-toll.aspx (stating that"[m]oney stress brought on by lighter paychecks this year is affecting more than Americans' wallets — it's taking a toll on their waistlines, friendships and sleep, according to results of a new survey fielded for the American Institute of CPAs by Harris Interactive).

[12] MetLife, Inc., 10th Annual Study of Employee Benefits Trends: Seeing Opportunity in Shifting Tides 51 (2012), available at http://www.winonaagency.com/img/~www.winonaagency.com/10th annual met life study of ee benefits trends.pdf ("22% of employees admit that they have taken unexpected time off in the past 12 months to deal with a financial issue and/or spent more time than they think they should at work on personal financial issues . . . ."). 15% of Gen Y respondents, 10% of Gen X respondents, 5% of Younger Boomer respondents, and 1% of Older Boomer respondents admitted to the same. Id. at 70.

[13] PricewaterhouseCoopers, LLC, supra note 5, at 10, 11.

[14] Men's Earnings at Peak at Age 45-54, U.S. Bureau of Labor Statistics (July 23, 1999), http://www.bls.gov/opub/ted/1999/Jul/wk3/art05.htm.

[15] PricewaterhouseCoopers, LLC, supra note 5, at 11.

[16] MetLife, Inc., supra note 12, at 3.

[17] Society for Human Resource Management, SHRM Research Spotlight: Financial Education Initiatives in the Workplace 2 (2012), available at http://www.shrm.org/Research/Survey Findings/Articles/Documents/Financial_Education_Flier_FINAL.PDF.

[18] Id.

[19] MetLife, Inc., supra note 12, at 13.

[20] Jennifer Robison, The Business Case for Wellbeing, Gallup Business Journal (June 9, 2010), http://businessjournal.gallup.com/content/139373/Business-Case-Wellbeing.aspx - 3.

[21] Financial Wellness: Waddell & Reed, Waddell & Reed, Inc., http://www.lincoln.wrfa.com/Financial-Wellness.6.htm (last visited Aug. 21, 2014).

[22] So-hyun Joo, Personal Financial Wellness and Worker Job Productivity, 47 (1998), available at http://scholar.lib.vt.edu/theses/available/etd-4198-155242/unrestricted/3.PDF.

[23] See, e.g., Financial Wellness | Student Wellness, The University of North Carolina at Chapel Hill, https://studentwellness.unc.edu/your-wellness/financial-wellness (last visited Aug. 21, 2014); What is Wellness? | Duke Student Affairs, Duke University, https://studentaffairs.duke.edu/duwell/about-us/what-wellness, (last visited Aug. 21, 2014).

[24] See MetLife, Inc., supra note 12, at 5.

[25] See, e.g., Kelly D. Edmiston et al., Weighing the Effects of Financial Education in the Workplace, Fed. Reserve Bank of Kan. City, 28 (2009), available at http://www.kansascityfed.org/publicat/cap/carwp09-01.pdf

[26] Several of the companies featured in this report noted that they became interested in adopting comprehensive financial wellness programs after noticing employees were making repeat visits to EAP programs designed for crisis management.

[27] Aon Hewitt, supra note 9.

[28] Soeren Mattke et al., Workplace Wellness Programs Study xiv (2013), available at http://www.dol.gov/ebsa/pdf/workplacewellnessstudyfinal.pdf.

[29] Stephen Miller, Study: Wellness Programs Saved $1 to $3 per Dollar Spent, Society for Human Resource Management (Sept. 12, 2012), http://www.shrm.org/hrdisciplines/benefits/articles/pages/wellness-dollars-saved.aspx; see Katherine Baicker et al., Workplace Wellness Programs can Generate Savings, 29 Health Affairs 304, 304 (2010), available at http://content.healthaffairs.org/content/29/2/304.full.

[30] Financial Finesse, a provider of financial wellness programs, reports one large employer found health care costs fell by 4.5% for participants in a financial wellness program compared to a 19.5% increase in costs for non-participants. See Financial Finesse, Inc., Actual Results from Company's Financial Wellness Program (2012), available at http://www.financialfinesse.com/wp-content/uploads/2014/07/ROI-Case-Study-08012013.pdf. For a general discussion of health wellness savings, see Health Policy Briefs, Health Affairs (May 16, 2013), http://www.healthaffairs.org/ healthpolicybriefs/brief.php?brief_id=93.

[31] See, e.g., Ralf Schwarzer et al., The Role of Stressful Life Events 26 (2001); Sheldon Cohen et al., Psychological Stress and Susceptibility to the Common Cold, 325 New England J. Medicine 606 (1991).

[32] American Psycholgy Association, supra note 5.

[33] Health Poll, AP-AOL/ABT SRBI (2008), available at http://surveys.ap.org/data/SRBI/AP-AOL Health Poll Topline 040808_FINAL_debt stress.pdf.

[34] Lucia F. Dunn & Ida A. Mirzaie, Working Paper, Determinants of Consumer Debt Stress: Differences by Debt Type and Gender (2012), available at http://www.chrr.osu.edu/content/surveys/cfm/doc/DSI-Working-Paper-07-19-12.pdf.

[35] AP-AOL/ABT SRBI, supra note 33.

[36] Ron Z. Goetzel et al., Ten Modifiable Health Risk Factors Are Linked To More Than One-Fifth Of Employer-Employee Health Care Spending, 31 Health Affairs 2474 (2012).

[37] Ron Z. Goetzel, et al., The relationship between modifiable health risks and health care expenditures, 40 J. Occup. Environ. Med. 843 (1998)(showing an analysis of the multi-employer HERO health risk and cost database).

[38] Goetzel et al., supra note 36, at 2481.

[39] Edmiston, supra note 25, at 19.

[40] For examples of definitions of employee engagement, see Towers Watson, 2012 Global Workforce Study: Engagement at Risk: Driving Strong Performance in a Volatile Global Environment 5 (2012); Rebecca L. Ray, et al., The Conference Board Inc., The State of Human Capital 2012: False Summit (2012); ADP, Inc., Employee Satisfaction vs. Employee Engagement: Are They the Same Thing? An ADP White Paper (2012).

[41] See, e.g., James Harter et al., Business-Unit-Level Relationships Between Employee Satisfaction, Employee Engagement , and Business Outcomes: A Meta-Analysis, 87 J. Applied Psychology 268 (2002).

[42] Ray et al., supra note 40, at 33.

[43] Tahira K. Hira and Cäzilia Loibl, Understanding the Impact of Employer-Provided Financial Education on Workplace Satisfaction, 39 J. Consumer Affairs 173, 185 (2005).

[44] Edmiston, supra note 25 at 19, 26.

[45] Charles Delafuente, Borrowing From the Future, New York Times (Feb. 11, 2013), http://www.nytimes.com/2013/02/12/business/early-withdrawals-plague-retirement-accounts-study-says.html?_r=0.

[46] Aon Hewitt, Leakage of Participants' DC Assets: How Loans, Withdrawals, and Cashouts Are Eroding Retirement Income (2011), available at http://www.aon.com/attachments/thought-leadership/survey_asset_leakage.pdf.

[47] Edmiston, supra note 25, at 17.

[48] See, e.g., United States Government Accountability Office, More DOD Actions Needed to Address Servicemembers' Personal Financial Management Issues (2005), available at http://www.gao.gov/assets/250/246138.pdf.

[49] William Skimmyhorn, Working Paper, Assessing Financial Education: Evidence from a Personal Financial Management Course 27 (2014).

[50] In a presentation at the CFPB, Professor Skimmyhorn cautioned the Army population may differ from the general workforce in some regards. For example, individuals who join the Army may be more likely to follow the directions of program instructors. It is also possible that many Army recruits are joining the service with the intention of improving their personal and financial situation. Even so, Skimmyhorn says the Army's results could suggest a similar course may benefit some employees.

[51] Baicker et al., supra note 29.

[52] PricewaterhouseCoopers, LLC., supra note 5, at 7.

[53] Robert L. Clark et al., Can Simple Informational Nudges Increase Employee Participation in a 401(k) Plan?, NBER Working Paper No. 19591 (2013).

[54] Annamaria Lusardi, Household Saving Behavior: The Role of Financial Literacy, Information, and Financial Education Programs, NBER Working Paper No. 13824 7 (2008).

[55] Telephone interview with Sally Hass (July 17, 2013).

[56] In a telephone interview and emails (February 2014), Sally Hass argued that employers have not maximized their current investments in financial education and have failed to shop for benefits providers or insist those providers actually meet education targets.

[57] Telephone interview with Sally Hass (July 17, 2013).

[58] Some of the employers contacted for this report reinforced the need to find low-cost or no-cost solutions to workplace financial education. For more on employer views on cost-effective solutions, see, for example, President's Advisory Council on Financial Capability Partnerships Committee, Workplace Financial Capability Framework – Summary of

Comments (2012), available at http://www.treasury.gov/resource-center/financial-education/Documents/PACFC Financial Capability at Work.pdf.

[59] *See id.* at 2.

[60] See, e.g., Daniel Fernandes et al., The Effect of Financial Literacy and Financial Education on Downstream Financial Behaviors (2013), available at http://www.nefe.org/Portals/0/WhatWeProvide/PrimaryResearch/PDF/CU%20Final%20Report.pdf

[61] Justine S. Hastings et al., Financial Literacy, Financial Education and Economic Outcomes, NBER Working Paper w18412 (2012), available at http://www.nber.org/papers/w18412.pdf.

[62] For an overall critique of financial literacy and financial literacy research, see generally Lauren E. Willis, Against Financial-Literacy Education, 94 U. Iowa L. Rev. 197 (2008), available at http://www.law.uiowa.edu/documents/ilr/willis.pdf.

[63] See, e.g., United States Government Accountability Office, A Federal Certification Process for Providers Would Pose Challenges 15-16 (2011); Fernandes et al., supra note 60, at 22.

[64] See Ian Hathaway & Sameer Khatiwada, Working Paper, Do Financial Education Programs Work? (2003); Patrick J. Bayer et al., The Effects of Financial Education in the Workplace: Evidence from a Survey of Employers, 47 Economic Inquiry 605 (2009).

[65] Telephone interview with QLI CEO Pat Kearns (Feb. 19, 2014).

[66] The Seattle-based company employs 350 people, most of them tasked with conducting telephone interviews on behalf of non-profits, government agencies, and public and private companies. Most of the employees at Pacific Research are low-to-moderate income. The survey industry is intensely competitive and faces pricing pressure both from lower cost states domestically and extremely low-cost competitors overseas.

[67] Interview with Tyler Phillips, Associate Director of Programs, Neighborhood Trust Financial Partners, (Aug. 14, 2013).

[68] Recent research has confirmed the important role that peer relationships play in influencing savings behavior at work. See, e.g., Esther Duflo & Emmanuel Saez, Participation and investment decisions in a retirement plan: the influence of colleague's choices, 85 J. Pub. Economics 121 (2002), available at elsa.berkeley.edu/users/saez/duflo.pdf.

[69] E-mail from Tyler Phillips, Associate Director of Programs, Neighborhood Trust Financial Partners (May, 5, 2014).

[70] The importance of peer influences in the Neighborhood Trust trainings are detailed in an e-email from Tyler Phillips, id.

[71] PricewaterhouseCoopers, LLC, supra note 5, at 8.

[72] D2D Fund, Inc., Can Games Build Financial Capability?: A Financial Entertainment Report (2012), available at http://www.d2dfund.org/files/publications/D2D_FE-Report_Pages_0.pdf.

[73] Nicholas W. Maynard et al., Can Games Build Financial Capability? 12 (2012),available at http://www.rand.org/content/dam/rand/pubs/working_papers/2012/RAND_WR963.pdf.

[74] Telephone interview with Alicia Elson, QLI Vice President of Human Resources (Oct. 11, 2013).

[75] Telephone Interview with Pat Kearns (Feb. 19, 2014).

[76] Turnover for Certified Nursing Assistants who provide direct patient care in long-term nursing facilities has been estimated at 65.6%. See American Health Care Association Department of Research, Report of Findings: 2007 AHCA Survey: National Staff Vacancy and Turnover in Nursing Facilities iii (2008), available at http://www.ahcancal.org/research_data/staffing/Documents/Vacancy_Turnover_Survey2007.pdf.

[77] NFM is now expanding, adding 2400 people with its expansion in Dallas area and plans to offer the program there after a transition period.

[78] E-mail from Steve Stokes, GCT Financial Wellness Coordinator (Apr. 25, 2014).

[79] Details of the Emergency Payroll Advance Program and a copy of the application were provided by e-mail from Steve Stokes, id.

[80] Aon plc – Investor Information – News Release, Aon Hewitt (May 24, 2011), http://ir.aon.com/phoenix.zhtml?c=105697&p=irol-newsArticle&id=1567166.

In: Financial Wellness in the Workplace
Editor: Wilfred O. Hunt
ISBN: 978-1-63463-179-2

Chapter 2

FINANCIAL CAPABILITY AT WORK: A STRATEGIC FRAMEWORK FOR EMPLOYERS*

President's Advisory Council on Financial Capability, Partnerships Committee

OVERVIEW

Background

The President's Advisory Council on Financial Capability (PACFC) believes that the workplace offers a critically important and trusted delivery point for financial education and related benefits, with the potential to positively impact as many as 138 million Americans.

* This is an edited, reformatted and augmented version of a President's Advisory Council on Financial Capability, Partnerships Committee publication, dated September 4, 2012.

Business Rationale

Increasingly, employers of all sizes are concluding that in order to be competitive, enhance productivity and drive employee retention, they want and need to provide financial education, benefits and resources that go beyond just saving for retirement.

- 76% of Americans say they are stressed about money.[1]
- 58% of employers say financial stress contributes to employee absences.[2]
- 78% of employers say employees are less productive at work when they are worried about personal financial issues. [2]
- Retirement experts generally recommend that individuals need between 70% and 80% of pre-retirement income – from a combination of sources including Social Security benefits, pensions, and personal savings – to achieve income adequacy in retirement.

The Challenge

The PACFC recommends that our nation's employers serve as leaders and role models by providing the five fundamentals – and working toward offering advanced features – to drive financial capability among America's workers.

Sources: [1] American Psychological Association Survey, 2010; [2] MetLife Study on Employee Benefits Trends, 2010.

Getting the Five Fundamentals in Place to Help Employees Improve Their Financial Outcomes

	Micro / Small Employers	Mid / Large Employers	Advanced Features
1 Benefits	Provide access to a retirement savings vehicle such as a SEP IRA, payroll deduction IRA, or SIMPLE IRA, preferably with an employer contribution and/or match. Also consider providing a defined benefit (e.g. multi-employer plan), profit sharing or low-cost defined contribution plan with the features recommended for Mid/Large Employers (at right).	Provide a defined benefit, profit sharing, or low-cost 401(k), 403(b), 457 defined contribution plan with the following features: -Auto-enrollment -Employer contributions -Default auto investment in professionally managed / appropriate asset allocation (such as target date fund, broad-based index ETF, etc.)	Enhanced defined contribution saving / investing features such as: - Auto-escalation of annual deferrals - Employer contribution regardless of employee participation - Auto enrollment for all employees (not just new hires) - Low-cost annuity investment option Supplementary defined benefit/contribution plan Investment guidance Financial assessment and one-on-one counseling
2 Educational resources	Provide opportunities for employees to learn from an objective source the core competencies of money management: - Budgeting - Saving / Goal setting - Borrowing / Debt management - Insurance / Income protection - Retirement planning / investing	Provide opportunities for employees to learn from an objective source the core competencies of money management: - Budgeting - Saving / Goal setting - Borrowing / Debt management - Insurance / Income protection - Retirement planning / investing	Additional educational topics to cover: - Buying a home - Saving for college - Getting ready to retire - Long term care Online tools and calculators
3 Marketing	Actively encourage employees to take advantage of the education and benefits. Employers should serve as visible champions of the efforts.	Create campaigns and communications that actively encourage employees to take advantage of the education and benefits. CEO / C-Suite leadership should serve as visible champions of the efforts.	- Multi-channel delivery (live, online) - Trigger-based messages (at birthdays, employment anniversaries, birth, etc.) - Family inclusion, testimonials and peer to-peer sharing - Manager engagement plan - Leverage employee diversity/resource groups
4 Measurement and metrics	Set specific, measurable goals and track progress. Key metrics include retirement savings plan participation and education participation.	Set specific, measurable goals and track progress at least annually. Key metrics include: 401(k) enrollment, deferral, diversification, balances and loans; educational participation; marketing results.	- Quarterly results summary / report - Segmented analysis by employee demographic - Dedicated staff and budget to implement program and track results
5 Products and services	Facilitate employee relationship with a bank or credit union by providing direct deposit.	Facilitate employee relationship with a bank or credit union by providing: - Direct deposit - Prescreened providers	- Negotiated preferred pricing / services - Enable direct deposit into multiple accounts, such as savings, 529, etc.

RESOURCES FOR EMPLOYERS*

AARP / FINRA / Retirement Security Project's Retirement Made Simpler	A coalition formed by AARP, the Financial Industry Regulatory Authority (FINRA) and the Retirement Security Project to provide companies with the tools, research and resources to make informed decisions about automating their retirement plans. Retirementmadesimpler.org
American Savings and Education Council / Employee Benefit Research Institute	ASEC is a nonprofit coalition of public and private organizations whose goal is to make saving and retirement planning a priority for all Americans. www.asec.org EBRI supports the development of sound employee benefits programs and public policy. www.ebri.org
Money Smart / Money Smart for Small Business	Created by the Federal Deposit Insurance Corporation (FDIC), Money Smart is a curriculum to help low- and moderate-income individuals improve their financial skills. They have also created a version of the program for small-business owners. fdic.gov/moneysmart
MyMoney.gov	MyMoney.gov is the federal government website featuring federal financial literacy and education programs, grants, and other consumer information, including information on Earned Income Tax Credit, health insurance and more. It is available in Spanish and English. www.mymoney.gov
National Endowment for Financial Education	- Resources on how to plan and deliver financial workshops: financialworkshopkits.org - Free beginner's guide to financial readiness: smartaboutmoney.org - Retirement resources for employees: myretirementpaycheck.org
NYSE / Financial Literacy Center Workplace Financial Fitness Kit	Online resources for employers and employees: nyse.nyx.com/financial-fitness-kit
Small Business Retirement Savings Advisor	Developed by the Department of Labor and Employee Benefits Security Administration, the Small Business Retirement Savings Advisor provides guidance about retirement savings options for small businesses. dol.gov/ebsa/publications/SEPPlans.html
Workplace Leaders in Financial Education Awards	Sponsored by Society for Human Resources Management and AICPA, the Workplace Leaders in Financial Education Award recognizes companies and institutions for exemplary financial literacy efforts: wlife.org/
World at Work	A nonprofit organization providing education, conferences and research focused on global human resources issues including compensation, benefits, work-life and integrated total rewards to attract, motivate and retain a talented workforce: worldatwork.org

* This list of objective, conflict-free resources is for reference only. It is not intended to be exhaustive. It does not endorse or promote specific initiatives, research, or organizations.

SUPPORTING RESEARCH*

401(k) Plans in Living Color: A Study of 401(k) Disparities Across Racial and Ethnic Groups	Headline: Study reveals retirement plans of African-Americans and Hispanics hit especially hard during tough economy: arielinvestments.com/401k-Study-2012/ Survey Sponsor: Ariel Investments and AON Hewitt. (April, 2012)
Help in Defined Contribution Plans: 2006 through 2010	Headline: 401(k) participants using professional investment help continue to do better than those who go it alone: aon.mediaroom.com/index.php?s=43&item=2388 Survey Sponsor: AON Hewitt and Financial Engines. (September, 2011)
The New Rules of Engagement for 401(k) Plans: Shifting Focus to Outcomes that Matter	Headline: Professional advice has a direct and positive impact on the behavior of 401(k) plan participants. www.aboutschwab.com/press/research/retirement_research/ Survey Sponsor: Charles Schwab, a 401(k) service provider to approximately 1.5 million company retirement plan participants. (September, 2010)
9th Annual Study of Employment Benefits Trends / Section 04: Remodeling the Benefits and Retirement Space	This broad-based survey on employee benefits contained several findings related to employees' financial health, including that employees with stressful financial situations report poorer health, and financial stress contributes to absenteeism and stifles on-the-job productivity. www.metlife.com/business/insights-and-tools/industry-knowledge/employee-benefits-trends-study/index.html#highlights Survey Sponsors: MetLife (March, 2011)
Financial Education: An Essential Component of Your Wellness Strategy	Headline: By offering broad-based financial advice and guidance, employers can help employees achieve their financial objectives and an overall sense of financial wellness. In turn, employers can profit from a more productive workforce and increase the appreciation of the benefits they provide. www.metlife.com/assets/institutional/services/insights-and-tools/cwb/ml-plansmart-whitepaper.pdf Survey Sponsor: MetLife (June, 2011)
Increasing the Effectiveness of Retirement Saving Programs for Females and Low Income Employees: A Marketing Approach	Headline: Effective employee communications programs can measurably reduce employee anxiety about retirement financial needs, and increase participation in and contributions to supplementary retirement accounts, compared to a control group. www.nefe.org/LinkClick.aspx?fileticket=HqSDPBWhVZk=&tabid=758 Authors: Annamaria Lusardi, Punam Keller, Adam Keller. Survey Sponsors: National Endowment for Financial Education, Dartmouth (April, 2009)

* This list of resources is for reference only. It is not intended to be exhaustive. It does not endorse or promote specific initiatives, research, or organizations.

In: Financial Wellness in the Workplace ISBN: 978-1-63463-179-2
Editor: Wilfred O. Hunt

Chapter 3

WORKPLACE FINANCIAL CAPABILITY FRAMEWORK – SUMMARY OF COMMENTS*

President's Advisory Council on Financial Capability Partnerships Committee

OVERVIEW

The President's Advisory Council on Financial Capability was created to advise the President and the Secretary of the Treasury on ways to assist the American people in understanding financial matters and making informed financial decisions. It is tasked with suggesting ways to coordinate and maximize the effectiveness of existing private and public sector efforts and identifying new approaches to increase financial capability through financial education and access to products and services.

One of the Council's areas of focus is enhancing the financial capability of America's workforce. The Council approved a recommendation in January geared toward improving financial capability for federal employees. We have now turned our attention to the private sector, and we hope to inspire employers across all industries to join us in this effort.

We seek to encourage employers of all shapes and sizes to adopt basic financial capability elements—and if they are already so engaged, to step up their offerings to more advanced services. These include a combination of

* This is an edited, reformatted and augmented version of a document issued in 2012.

benefits, educational resources, products and services, motivating communications, and metrics for measuring outcomes.

In its May 2012 white paper, "Every American Financially Empowered: A Guide to Increasing Financial Capability Among Students, Workers and Residents in Communities," the White House included a one-page "Employer Checklist" of steps employers can take to improve the financial capability of their employees. The Council's Partnerships Subcommittee has developed an implementation framework to supplement the White House publication in order to more fully support and expand financial capability opportunities in the workplace.

"Financial Capability at Work: A Strategic Framework to Guide Employers" ("Framework") was developed over the past year with significant input from business leaders, employee groups, union leaders, researchers, policy experts, government and nonprofit leaders, human resources and benefits experts and many others. This early guidance took the form of numerous phone interviews and discussions, listening sessions and informal meetings. The PACFC used the input to shape an initial draft document. This draft was publicly released through more than 300 stakeholders for additional feedback and input from September through mid-October, 2012. Thirty-four executive-level stakeholders responded to the following questions:

- Are these elements realistic and achievable for employers to implement?
- What would motivate or inspire your organization to adopt these elements?
- Are there best practices you can share? Are there challenges?

This report provides a high-level summary of that feedback, grouped by key themes. The detailed feedback will be made available on the U.S. Department of Treasury's website.

FEEDBACK SUMMARY

Overall, respondents supported the concept of promoting financial capability in the workplace and encouraging employers to do more to help improve their employees' financial outcomes. They responded positively to the Framework structure, as well as the five key elements proposed. Several key themes and recommendations emerged in the individual responses:

Overall, the Framework Is Realistic and Achievable for Mid- and Large-Size Employers

- The vast majority of respondents – who largely represented mid- or large-sized employers – expressed that they already offer many of the elements in their size category, including some elements from the "advanced features."
- One respondent recommended that the Framework add an element or recast the Framework organization around the concept of *retirement adequacy*, or the extent to which all the retirement plans for a workforce, taken as a whole and in combination with Social Security benefits, are expected to deliver "adequate income" in retirement.
- Another recommended including more guidance for helping employers connect employees with products and services, as well as resources to help benefits professionals with turn-key implementation. But in contradictory feedback, other respondents expressed concern about employer liability in endorsing or partnering with particular service providers.
- Several respondents recommended connecting employers with financial capability programming that is easy to adopt, such as services offered by third-party providers who manage all aspects of the program for the benefits administrator. These are much more appealing – according to research by the New America Foundation – than programs the employer must manage internally. (This applies to micro- and small-sized employers as well.)

Every Employer Is Different, and the Framework Allows for Flexibility to Satisfy Employers' Varied Needs and Circumstances

- A nonprofit global human resources association commended the Framework for allowing employers to retain the flexibility to design programs that best satisfy the needs of their employees.

- Some respondents indicated that a stronger emphasis could be placed on the notion of leveraging internal and external resources to accomplish the initiative laid out in the Framework. For example, the Framework could specifically encourage employers to tap into community resources, national campaigns (i.e. America Saves, ChooseToSave.org, etc.), and their existing benefits providers to bring financial education into the workforce at minimal or no cost.

Implementation May Be Challenging for Micro- and Small-Size Employers

- Respondents were mixed on whether the framework would be achievable for small and micro businesses. A handful of respondents expressed concern that small businesses may find the elements either too financially burdensome to implement, or too difficult to implement due to lack of infrastructure or staff.

The Council Should Clarify That the Framework Is Not Intended as a Government Mandate

- Several respondents were concerned about the possibility of the Framework becoming a government mandate, and recommended the paper clearly state that the Council is not recommending a new government mandate for employers.
- One respondent indicated that obtaining financial education is the responsibility of the employee, not the employer. This respondent also encouraged individuals to look to local nonprofit organizations for such help.
- Several respondents indicated that the Framework should clearly state that the Council views workplace financial capability efforts as voluntary, and that it should encourage government leaders to maintain policies that ensure they remain so.

Employers May Need More Clarification Around Fiduciary Responsibility and Risk of Liability

- Respondents stated that fiduciary responsibility is a barrier to employers in terms of offering financial education or guidance.
- They recommend the Council explicitly address fears about increased liability, and recommended that the Framework point to government resources that clarify safe harbor around this issue.
- One respondent recommended expanding the Department of Labor's Interpretive Bulletin 96-1 (IB 96-1) in defining the educational information employers can provide without risk of liability.

The Types of Financial Benefits and Educational Resources Could Go Even Further

- Several respondents encouraged inclusion of income protection benefits, such as disability insurance and health insurance, in the "Employer-sponsored savings vehicles" section.
- Several respondents encouraged inclusion of information on access to credit counseling services.
- Many respondents noted that while budgeting is called out as an educational topic, the Framework could do more to promote budgeting skills and help facilitate emergency or "rainy day" funds for employees.
- One respondent recommended that the benefits section be expanded to be more relevant to employers who provide employees with defined benefit plans. They argued, for example, that the "Measurement and Metrics" element provided examples that relate primarily to defined contribution plans, and do not adequately apply to defined benefit plans.
- One respondent recommended that the term "conflict-free" be added to modify educational offerings as well as benefits such as "[f]inancial assessment and one-on-one counseling."

Financial Incentives Could Be Effective in Motivating Employers to Offer Financial Education and Benefits

- Several respondents encouraged the Council to recommend that the government create financial incentives to help defray the cost of implementation of new benefits and education, and to motivate more employers to consider expanding their offerings.

RESPONDENTS' SUMMARY COMMENTS

	Respondent	*Key Themes*
1	AFL-CIO	• Recommend the Framework define success for employers' retirement education and benefits plans by whether the employers' workers are expected to have enough in retirement (retirement adequacy). • Recommend the Framework be more relevant to workers covered by defined benefit plans. • Ensure that all the recommendations in the Framework clarify that education, advice and guidance must be conflict free.
2	U.S. Chamber of Commerce	• The Chamber expressed that many of its members are already implementing on the five key elements, and that many of its members do even more. • Consider encouraging employers to offer benefits that help workers protect against loss of income due to illness or injury. • Clarify that the private retirement system must remain voluntary, and that the PACFC believes employers should be encouraged – not mandated – to provide opportunities for retirement savings. • Address employers' fears about increased liability due to providing financial education. Employers rely heavily on Department of Labor Interpretive Bulletin 96-1 (IB 96-1) in defining the educational information they provide without fear of liability. The Chamber recommends expanding IB 96-1 to allow employers to provide educational information without it being considered investment advice.
3	Capital Area Asset Builders	• The Framework is a great start for bringing financial education and resources into the workplace. • For employers that offer Employee Assistance Programs (EAPs), resources for financial assistance could be included as an offering toward overall wellbeing. • Be sure to provide education and resources in multiple languages if the employee demographics necessitate it. • The government or this Framework resource list could include a list of local organizations by state that offer financial wellness programs employers could tap into. The list could include both nonprofit and for-profit organizations.
4	World at Work	• The Framework "supports a holistic approaching, by addressing many fundamental practices that can lead to improved employee financial

	Respondent	*Key Themes*
		outcomes … The suggested initiatives within the umbrella of the five fundamentals cited in the framework are most certainly realistic and achievable for employers to implement." • Every employer has unique workforce demographics with unique employee needs. The flexibility of the Framework is therefore very important. • Consider making a stronger recommendation for employers to leverage both internal and external resources to accomplish initiatives outlined in the framework. Often times employers can tap into community resources, regional and national campaigns, and resources from existing vendors to bring financial education to the workforce and minimal or no cost.
5	Prudential Financial	• In general the Framework is realistic and achievable for employers, but there are challenges with certain elements, particularly for micro/small employers. Specifically: • It does not seem realistic for micro/small employers to offer a defined benefit plan, given the financial and administrative hurdles. In fact, even among many medium to large employers, defined benefit plans have been steadily decreasing. • The term "investment guidance" needs further clarification, given that some employers define the term very narrowly. Similarly, one-one-one counseling may not be achievable for many employers. • The "low cost annuity option" seems like an odd addition, given that all categories should assume reasonably priced, appropriate investment options. • Promoting "pre-screened providers" seems problematic – who would develop the criteria? Who would monitor the provider to ensure continued alignment? If there was a negative outcome with the provider, would the employer be accountable? • Prudential has already implemented most of the elements of the Framework in an effort to attract and retain the best talent. Talent acquisition and retention could be called out as a stronger motivator / incentive for employers. • The Federal government could play a role in championing and promoting the Framework.
6	JP Morgan Chase	• Framework is realistic and achievable for mid-/large-sized employers like JP Morgan Chase (200k+ U.S. employees). The already offers most of the elements in the framework. • The respondent shared "best practices" including o Providing targeted communications with customized information about each employee's situation (i.e., show specific dollar amounts an employee gave up in 401(k) match to encourage enrollment or increased contributions. o Providing the same communications via multiple channels and touchpoints.

(Continued)

	Respondent	Key Themes
7	Office of Financial Empowerment (OFE) City of San Francisco (Note: The San Francisco OFE co-chairs the Cities for Financial Empowerment, a network of various sized cities across the nation representing 19 million people.)	• Framework is compelling and achievable for both large and small employers, and is presented in a concise, straightforward manner. • The overall message could be strengthened by extending beyond education and highlighting ways in which employers can provide employees direct access to safe financial products. • The terminology for the five fundamentals could be revised to better align with employee benefits professionals. For example, change "Benefits" to "Retirement Savings" and "Education Resources" to "Financial Education". • Provide accompanying documents that help benefits professionals with clear actions and next steps for implementation. • Clarify that the audience for this document. (CEOs, Human Resources staff, etc) • Address employer resistance by putting a greater emphasis on rewards and benefits to employers. For example, direct deposit helps employees, but also reduces employer costs related to payroll printing, processing and administration. • The comments shared resources such as the organizations white paper on Financial Empowerment through Employer Engagement.
8	New America Foundation	• The organization is currently engaged in research that seeks to catalogue financial capability programs currently offered by employers and document experiences with implementing such programs. Based on that research, they recommend the following: • Add "Gauge employee financial needs and concerns" and "Bring the right stakeholders on board" to the top of the Employer Checklist. • Add access to non-retirement, liquid savings vehicles and emergency financial assistance to the list of products and services available through the workplace. • Make centralizing information on financial capability programming a priority in marketing, and consider increasing the importance of testimonials and peer-to-peer sharing beyond an "advanced feature". • Connect employers with financial capability programming that is easy to adopt, such as services offered by third-party providers who manage all aspects of the program for the benefits administrator. These are much more appealing – according to NAF research – than programs the employer must manage internally.
9	Arkansas Federal Credit Union	• The elements are realistic for mid- to large-employers, and the organization supports the fundamentals laid out in the framework. • Micro- and small employers could be challenged in time and with competing priorities to implement it. (The organization works with a number of small employers who often do not share or implement even the free educational resources provided to them for their employees.)

	Respondent	Key Themes
10	EMSC	• From an employer perspective, the framework needs a stronger rationale for return on investment. • Educational and marketing recommendations should be packaged and turn-key for implementation in the workplace. • The firm would be motivated to adopt the recommendations under the following circumstance: "if we meet certain metrics (tbd), we could get a pass or exception on our annual 401(k) non-discrimination testing." For some companies, "making our plan safe harbor is cost prohibitive
11	Wisconsin Dept. of Transportation Employee Assistance Program	• Framework levels are reasonable in most settings. • The greatest barrier to implementation for employers is time and money. • Provides a testimonial for the success and effectiveness of the "Investor Education in Your Workplace ®" program from the Investor Protection Institute. • Provides research results on employees' positive behavioral changes after having gone through the program.
12	Aetna	• Aetna's program includes most of the elements in the framework, so the company sees them as "realistic and achievable." • Aetna offered "best practice" guiding principles: o One size does not fit all. Be willing to customize for target audiences. o If it doesn't work, change it. o People did not get into financial trouble over night. They will not get out of it over night. Give the program time to work. o Be "unbiased, unbiased, unbiased." o Use multimedia, i.e. webcasts, video, in person workshops, newsletters, intranet. Different people have different learning styles. • Challenges employers should consider when implementing programs: o Employees finding time in their work day to take advantage. o Manager engagement. o Finding unbiased education in the employees' best interest.
13	Host Hotels & Resorts	• The format is good. • Including terminology around "defined benefits" could "scare off" some companies, so be clearer about what is intended and consider providing information on cost. • Large organizations will fall into a number of sub categories that will require different tools and techniques. For example, a large technical workforce is very different from a retail workforce with many hourly and part-time workers. • Provider an executive summary of the best supporting research available to help the human resources teams who likely be implementing.
14	Unum	• Unum strongly encourages including insurance / income protection in the benefits portion of the five fundamentals. • Attached Harvard Business Review study indicating 80% of employers say income-protection benefits play a role in attracting and retaining top talent and increasing productivity. • Attached supporting documentation indicating that the Consumer Federation of America believes financial capability would be increased if income protection were more prevalent, and that employers have an important role to play in providing access to it.

(Continued)

	Respondent	Key Themes
15	Bank of America	• The elements are realistic and achievable to implement "over time." • The primary motivator for BofA to adopt and/or further support initiatives would be employee requests. • One challenge in driving employee adoption of such programs is building awareness among employees of the benefits and educational programs the company offers.
16	HNTB	• The Framework is a thoughtful challenge to employers, but it should not be presented as a mandate. • Auto-enrollment is not practical for all employers. • Plan sponsors could be highlighted as resources for financial literacy education vs. individual company-created campaigns. • The government needs to address potential liability for providing what could be construed as financial advice under ERISA.
17	Bank of NY Mellon	• The Framework is realistic and achievable for an employer of BNY Mellon's size. • Consider recommending employers also leverage publicly available, objective free tools and educational resources when possible. • BNY Mellon supports the business rationale for providing the framework elements: "By providing financial tools and knowledge to their employees, businesses can help to increase employee retention and employee engagement; increase productivity; improve an employee's quality of life by eliminating financial stressors...." • Best practices suggested: Provide employees with one-on-one financial planning sessions, and an online "financial wellness" portal where they can easily access budgeting tools, information, and assistance in the event of personal financial crisis. • The greatest challenge is getting employees to use all the benefits and resources available to them.
18	Associated Estates	• Recommends adding the following to the framework; saving for college / 529s; income-tax planning; estate planning; long-term care planning.
19	NestWise	• The needs of the employer and incentives for success need more consideration. • Several challenges for employers: o Especially small employers may not have financial expertise. o Small employers may not have benefits staff. How can we make this more manageable for employers and their staff? o Deep concern about fiduciary responsibility and risk. o Employers are wary to make product recommendations / choices for employees – they are concerned about liability.
20	Investor Protection Trust and Investor Protection Institute	• Recommends recognition, rewards, competitions and simple / easy-to-implement programs as a way to motivate employers to do more. • Provided an overview of the "Investor Education in the Workplace®" program, along with research supporting its effectiveness in motivating behavioral change among employees. • Provided research entitled "Investor Education for Credit Union Employees: Survey Results for Wisconsin."

	Respondent	Key Themes
21	Evraz North America	• The five elements are realistic and achievable. • A best-practice they employ is auto-enrollment at 5%, match the 5% dollar for dollar, and then add 3% on top of the match. This results in very high participation rates.
22	Sharp Electronics	• The document is well-crafted. • It has a wealth of information.
23	Navy Federal Credit Union	• The elements on the Framework are "absolutely realistic for employers to implement for both Micro/Small Employers and Mid/Large Employers" • The Navy Federal Credit Union already offers all the framework elements for Mid/Large Employers and most of the "Advanced Features" • Best practices include: o 410(k) with 100% match up to 6% o A company-paid defined benefit pension o A quarterly total rewards statement with links to external sources like Choosetosave.org, SSA.gov, and Medicare.gov o Planning aids and modelers to help with retirement planning and managing flexible spending accounts. o Educational programs on basic finance topics plus first-time homebuyer seminars. o Real-estate assistance program, loan discount program, identity theft protection program, and much more. • The greatest challenges for employers will be cost, workload, encouraging and sustaining employee participation, reaching Gen Y and/or creating materials and programs that speak to multiple generations at very different stages of financial wellbeing. • The Advisory Council should consider developing a basic presentation for employers to modify or use "off-the-shelf" for financial education.
24	MassMutual Financial Group	• Starting with the Framework's five fundamentals is a great way to present best practices for employers while illustrating the range of options and features available to help employees improve their financial outcomes. • Retirement plan providers can and do play an important role in helping employers deliver fundamental components of the Framework. Specific ways in which they can help include: o Helping the employer establish a plan, based on company size, industry, employee demographics and employer goals. o Providing education to participants. o Implementing personalized awareness and marketing campaigns. o Assisting with setting and executing measures of success.
25	Belvoir Federal Credit Union	• Framework is well-thought-out and "visionary."
26	BB&T	• The Framework is realistic and achievable, and many companies have been working for years to encourage employees to utilize their benefits and take advantage of educational offerings. • BB&T integrates its financial wellness programs into an overall "wellness" approach, including Career Wellbeing, Financial Wellbeing, Physical Wellbeing, and Community Wellbeing.

(Continued)

	Respondent	Key Themes
27	InCharge Education Foundation	• Framework should focus more on getting people "investment ready" (debt reduction, credit improvement, emergency funds) before leaping to retirement planning. • Consider including education on credit scores and credit reports. • Move educational resources for "buying a home" from Advanced to Micro/Small and Mid/Large sections. • Educational programs need incentives to encourage participation.
28	Scott Credit Union	• Framework is good. • Cultural change is required for employers to offer more benefits and for employees to take advantage of them. • Explore incentives for businesses to offer such plans and programs • Consider tracking business results of employers that offer programs, to more concretely demonstrate business value. • Employers should do more to demonstrate the value of participation to employees– help them see the tangible benefits.
29	TIAA-CREF Financial Services	• The Framework is realistic and achievable, and these recommendations are "essential." • This could be a first step toward a new approach to retirement readiness in which it is a shared responsibility between employers and employees; a system that provides income that can last a lifetime; that helps retirees meet their uninsured healthcare expenses; and is delivered in a tailored way (not one-size-fits-all) that meets peoples' individual needs. • People at different ages and income levels have different needs, as do women. A new national approach to retirement readiness should address this. • One of the most pressing challenges is helping people prepare for and achieve lifetime income during retirement, now that retirement can stretch for decades. Offering education and products to help achieve this is critical.
30	Service Credit Union	• Framework is good, and the respondent's organization already offers the five elements. • Recommends promoting the Simple IRA to employers who cannot afford or manage a 401(k). • Promote employee thrift by setting up a separate "rainy day" account. • Promote the use of flexible spending accounts and dependent care accounts.
31	Fort Knox FCU	• Recommends more employers consider offering defined benefit programs.
32	1st Advantage FCU	• Framework is good, and the respondent's organization already offers the five elements. • 1st Advantage also offers a full-time budget and credit counselor, providing free consultation to employees and members. • 1st Advantage links health and wellness education with financial education and assistance for a comprehensive employee wellness program.

	Respondent	Key Themes
33	Pentagon Federal Credit Union (PenFed)	• While the organization has a 401(k) and offers a match to its employees, the respondent believes the government should not mandate required employer matching. • The organization supports the framework proposal; however, "absent required financial education courses in high school and college, the ability of these programs to enjoy their full potential will be limited." • "For this program to reach its full potential, we need to mandate school systems to teach financial literacy."
34	First Light FCU	• Framework is good, and the respondent's organization already offers the five elements. • Suggests adding resources for credit counseling and budgeting. • Suggests employee incentives for meeting financial goals.

ACKNOWLEDGMENTS

In addition to the organizations who responded to the PACFC's request for feedback (summarized on the previous pages of this document), the PACFC Partnerships Subcommittee would like to acknowledge the following organizations, whose executives and staff provided direct guidance and feedback through numerous meetings, calls, and email correspondences:

American Institute of Certified Public Accountants
Best Buy
Boys & Girls Clubs of America
Charles Schwab & Co., Inc.
Cities for Financial Empowerment
Clinton Global Initiative
Delaware Financial Empowerment Partnership
E-Trade
Employee Benefits Research Institute
Financial Literacy Center
Gap Inc.
HR Policy Institute
HelloWallet
McDonald's
Men's Warehouse
NASDAQ OMX
National Federation of Independent Businesses
National League of Cities
Nationwide

New York Stock Exchange Foundation
San Francisco 49ers
SCPMG-Kaiser
Sharp Electronics
Silicon Valley Group
Society for Human Resources Management
Taco Bell / Yum Brands
Toyota
United Way of Delaware
United Way of San Francisco
U.S. Department of Treasury, Office of Consumer Policy
Visa

In: Financial Wellness in the Workplace
Editor: Wilfred O. Hunt
ISBN: 978-1-63463-179-2

Chapter 4

SAVING AND INVESTING: A ROADMAP TO YOUR FINANCIAL SECURITY THROUGH SAVING AND INVESTING*

Securities and Exchange Commission, Office of Investor Education and Advocacy

While money doesn't grow on trees, it can grow when you save and invest wisely.

Knowing how to secure your financial well-being is one of the most important things you'll ever need in life. You don't have to be a genius to do it. You just need to know a few basics, form a plan, and be ready to stick to it. No matter how much or little money you have, the important thing is to educate yourself about your opportunities. In this publication, we'll cover the basics on saving and investing.

At the SEC, we enforce the laws that determine how investments are offered and sold to you. These laws protect investors, but you need to do your part, too. Part of this publication tells you how to check out investments and the people that sell them so you do not fall victim to fraud or costly mistakes.

No one can guarantee that you'll make money from investments you make. But if you get the facts about saving and investing and follow through

* This is an edited, reformatted and augmented version of a publication, SEC Pub. 009 (06/11), issued June 2011.

with an intelligent plan, you should be able to gain financial security over the years and enjoy the benefits of managing your money.

Please feel free to contact us with any of your questions or concerns about investing. It always pays to learn before you invest. And congratulations on taking your first step on the road to financial security!

U.S. Securities and Exchange Commission
Office of Investor Education and Advocacy
100 F Street, N.E.
Washington, D.C. 20549-0213
Toll-free: (800) SEC-0330
Website: www.investor.gov

DON'T WAIT TO GET STARTED

You Can Do It! It's Easier Than You Think

No one is born knowing how to save or to invest. Every successful investor starts with the basics—the information in this publication.

A few people may stumble into financial security—a wealthy relative may die, or a business may take off. But for most people, the only way to attain financial security is to save and invest over a long period of time.

Time after time, people of even modest means who begin the journey reach financial security and all that it promises: buying a home, educational opportunities for their children, and a comfortable retirement. If they can do it, so can you!

KEYS TO FINANCIAL SUCCESS

1. Make a financial plan.
2. Pay off any high interest debts.
3. Start saving and investing as soon as you've paid off your debts.

Your First Step—Making a Financial Plan

What Are the Things You Want to Save and Invest for?

- a home
- a car
- an education
- a comfortable retirement
- your children
- medical or other emergencies
- periods of unemployment
- caring for parents

Make your own list and then think about which goals are the most important to you. List your most important goals first. Decide how many years you have to meet each specific goal, because when you save or invest you'll need to find a savings or investment option that fits your time frame for meeting each goal. Many tools exist to help you put your financial plan together. You'll find a wealth of information, including calculators and links to non-commercial resources at www.investor.gov.

YOUR FINANCIAL GOALS

If you don't know where you are going, you may end up somewhere you don't want to be. To end up where you want to be, you'll need a roadmap, a financial plan.

What do you want to save or invest for?	By when?
1. ______________________	______
2. ______________________	______
3. ______________________	______
4. ______________________	______
5. ______________________	______

Know Your Current Financial Situation

Sit down and take an honest look at your entire financial situation. You can never take a journey without knowing where you're starting from, and a journey to financial security is no different. You'll need to figure out on paper your current situation—what you own and what you owe. You'll be creating a "net worth statement." On one side of the page, list what you own. These are your "assets." And on the other side list what you owe other people, your "liabilities" or debts.

YOUR NET WORTH STATEMENT			
Assets	**Current Value**	**Liabilities**	**Amount**
Cash	______	Mortgage balance	______
Checking accounts	______	Credit cards	______
Savings	______	Bank loans	______
Cash value of life insurance	______	Car loans	______
Retirement accounts	______	Student loans	______
Real estate	______	Other	______
Home	______		______
Other investments	______		______
Personal property	______		______
TOTAL	______	**TOTAL**	______

Subtract your liabilities from your assets. If your assets are larger than your liabilities, you have a "positive" net worth. If your liabilities are greater than your assets, you have a "negative" net worth.

You'll want to update your "net worth statement" every year to keep track of how you are doing. Don't be discouraged if you have a negative net worth. If you follow a plan to get into a positive position, you're doing the right thing.

Know Your Income and Expenses

The next step is to keep track of your income and your expenses for every month. Write down what you and others in your family earn, and then your monthly expenses.

Pay Yourself or Your Family First

Include a category for savings and investing. What are you paying yourself every month?

Many people get into the habit of saving and investing by following this advice: always pay yourself or your family first. Many people find it easier to pay themselves first if they allow their bank to automatically remove money from their paycheck and deposit it into a savings or investment account.

Likely even better, for tax purposes, is to participate in an employer-sponsored retirement plan such as a 401(k), 403(b), or 457(b). These plans will typically not only automatically deduct money from your paycheck, but will immediately reduce the taxes you are paying. Additionally, in many plans the employer matches some or all of your contribution. When your employer does that, it's offering "free money."

Any time you have automatic deductions made from your paycheck or bank account, you'll increase the chances of being able to stick to your plan and to realize your goals.

Finding Money to Save or Invest

If you are spending all your income, and never have money to save or invest, you'll need to look for ways to cut back on your expenses. When you watch where you spend your money, you will be surprised how small everyday expenses that you can do without add up over a year.

KNOW YOUR INCOME AND WHAT YOU SPEND	
Monthly Income	________
Monthly Expenses	
Savings	________
Investments	________
Housing	________
Rent or mortgage	________
Electricity	________
Gas/oil	________
Telephone	________
Water/sewer	________
Property tax	________
Furniture	________
Food	________
Transportation	________
Loans	________
Insurance	________
Education	________
Recreation	________
Child care	________
Health care	________
Gifts	________
Other	________
TOTAL	________

Small Savings Add up to Big Money

How Much Does a Cup of Coffee Cost You?

If you buy a cup of coffee every day for $1.00 (an awfully good price for a decent cup of coffee, nowadays), that adds up to $365.00 a year. If you saved that $365.00 for just one year, and put it into a savings account or investment that earns 5% a year, it would grow to $465.84 by the end of 5 years, and by the end of 30 years, to $1,577.50.

That's the power of"compounding." With compound interest, you earn interest on the money you save and on the interest that money earns. Over time, even a small amount saved can add up to big money.

If you are willing to watch what you spend and look for little ways to save on a regular schedule, you can make money grow. You just did it with one cup of coffee.

If a small cup of coffee can make such a huge difference, start looking at how you could make your money grow if you decided to spend less on other things and save those extra dollars.

If you buy on impulse, make a rule that you'll always wait 24 hours to buy anything. You may lose your desire to buy it after a day. And try emptying your pockets and wallet of spare change at the end of each day. You'll be surprised how quickly those nickels and dimes add up!

Pay Off Credit Card or Other High Interest Debt

Speaking of things adding up, few investment strategies pay off as well as, or with less risk than, merely paying off all high interest debt you may have.

Many people have wallets filled with credit cards, some of which they've "maxed out" (meaning they've spent up to their credit limit). Credit cards can make it seem easy to buy expensive things when you don't have the cash in your pocket—or in the bank. But credit cards aren't free money.

Most credit cards charge high interest rates—as much as 18 percent or more—if you don't pay off your balance in full each month. If you owe money on your credit cards, the wisest thing you can do is pay off the balance in full as quickly as possible. Virtually no investment will give you the high returns you'll need to keep pace with an 18 percent interest charge. That's why you're better off eliminating all credit card debt before investing savings.

Once you've paid off your credit cards, you can budget your money and begin to save and invest. Here are some tips for avoiding credit card debt:

Put Away the Plastic

Don't use a credit card unless your debt is at a manageable level and you know you'll have the money to pay the bill when it arrives.

Know What You Owe

It's easy to forget how much you've charged on your credit card. Every time you use a credit card, write down how much you have spent and figure out how much you'll have to pay that month. If you know you won't be able to pay your balance in full, try to figure out how much you can pay each month and how long it'll take to pay the balance in full.

Pay Off the Card with the Highest Rate

If you've got unpaid balances on several credit cards, you should first pay down the card that charges the highest rate. Pay as much as you can toward that debt each month until your balance is once again zero, while still paying the minimum on your other cards.

The same advice goes for any other high interest debt (about 8% or above) which does not offer the tax advantages of, for example, a mortgage.

Now, once you have paid off those credit cards and begun to set aside some money to save and invest, what are your choices?

MAKING MONEY GROW

The Two Ways to Make Money

There are basically two ways to make money.

1. You work for money.
Someone pays you to work for them or you have your own business.
2. Your money works for you.
You take your money and you save or invest it.

Your Money Can Work for You in Two Ways

Your money earns money. When your money goes to work, it may earn a steady paycheck. Someone pays you to use your money for a period of time. When you get your money back, you get it back plus "interest." Or, if you buy stock in a company that pays "dividends" to shareholders, the company may pay you a portion of its earnings on a regular basis. Your money can make an "income," just like you. You can make more money when you and your money work.

You buy something with your money that could increase in value. You become an owner of something that you hope increases in value over time. When you need your money back, you sell it, hoping someone else will pay you more for it. For instance, you buy a piece of land thinking it will increase in value as more businesses or people move into your town. You expect to sell the land in five, ten, or twenty years when someone will buy it from you for a lot more money than you paid.

And sometimes, your money can do both at the same time— earn a steady paycheck and increase in value.

The Differences between Saving and Investing

Saving

Your "savings" are usually put into the safest places, or products, that allow you access to your money at any time. Savings products include savings accounts, checking accounts, and certificates of deposit. Some deposits in these products may be insured by the Federal Deposit Insurance Corporation or the National Credit Union Administration. But there's a tradeoff for security and ready availability. Your money is paid a low wage as it works for you.

After paying off credit cards or other high interest debt, most smart investors put enough money in a savings product to cover an emergency, like sudden unemployment. Some make sure they have up to six months of their income in savings so that they know it will absolutely be there for them when they need it.

But how "safe" is a savings account if you leave all of your money there for a long time, and the interest it earns doesn't keep up with inflation? What if you save a dollar when it can buy a loaf of bread. But years later when you withdraw that dollar plus the interest you earned on it, it can only buy half a loaf? This is why many people put some of their money in savings, but look to investing so they can earn more over long periods of time, say three years or longer.

Investing

When you "invest," you have a greater chance of losing your money than when you "save." The money you invest in securities, mutual funds, and other similar investments typically is not federally insured. You could lose your "principal"—the amount you've invested. But you also have the opportunity to earn more money.

THE BASIC TYPES OF PRODUCTS	
Savings	**Investments**
Savings accounts	Bonds
Certificates of deposit	Stocks
Checking accounts	Mutual funds
	Real estate
	Commodities (gold, silver, etc.)

What About Risk?

All investments involve taking on risk. It's important that you go into any investment in stocks, bonds or mutual funds with a full understanding that you could lose some or all of your money in any one investment. While over the long term the stock market has historically provided around 10% annual returns (closer to 6% or 7% "real" returns when you subtract for the effects of inflation), the long term does sometimes take a rather long, long time to play out. Those who invested all of their money in the stock market at its peak in 1929 (before the stock market crash) would wait over 20 years to see the stock market return to the same level.

However, those that kept adding money to the market throughout that time would have done very well for themselves, as the lower cost of stocks in the 1930s made for some hefty gains for those who bought and held over the course of the next twenty years or more.

It is often said that the greater the risk, the greater the potential reward in investing, but taking on unnecessary risk is often avoidable. Investors best protect themselves against risk by spreading their money among various investments, hoping that if one investment loses money, the other investments will more than make up for those losses. This strategy, called " diversification," can be neatly summed up as, "Don't put all your eggs in one basket." Investors also protect themselves from the risk of investing all their money at the wrong time (think 1929) by following a consistent pattern of adding new money to their investments over long periods of time.

Once you've saved money for investing, consider carefully all your options and think about what diversification strategy makes sense for you. While the SEC cannot recommend any particular investment product, you should know that a vast array of investment products exists—including stocks and stock mutual funds, corporate and municipal bonds, bond mutual funds, certificates of deposit, money market funds, and U.S. Treasury securities.

Diversification can't ***guarantee*** that your investments won't suffer if the market drops. But it can improve the chances that you won't lose money, or that if you do, it won't be as much as if you weren't diversified.

What Are the Best Investments for Me?

The answer depends on when you will need the money, your goals, and if you will be able to sleep at night if you purchase a risky investment where you could lose your principal.

For instance, if you are saving for retirement, and you have 35 years before you retire, you may want to consider riskier investment products, knowing that if you stick to only the "savings" products or to less risky investment products, your money will grow too slowly—or, given inflation and taxes, you may ***lose*** the purchasing power of your money. A frequent mistake people make is putting money they will not need for a very long time in investments that pay a low amount of interest.

On the other hand, if you are saving for a short-term goal, five years or less, you don't want to choose risky investments, because when it's time to sell, you may have to take a loss. Since investments often move up and down in value rapidly, you want to make sure that you can wait and sell at the best possible time.

What Are Investments All About?

When you make an investment, you are giving your money to a company or enterprise, hoping that it will be successful and pay you back with even more money.

Stocks and Bonds

Many companies offer investors the opportunity to buy either stocks or bonds. The example below shows you how stocks and bonds differ.

Let's say you believe that a company that makes automobiles may be a good investment. Everyone you know is buying one of its cars, and your friends report that the company's cars rarely break down and run well for years. You either have an investment professional investigate the company and read as much as possible about it, or you do it yourself.

After your research, you're convinced it's a solid company that will sell many more cars in the years ahead.

The automobile company offers both stocks and bonds. With the bonds, the company agrees to pay you back your initial investment in ten years, plus pay you interest twice a year at the rate of 8% a year.

If you buy the stock, you take on the risk of potentially losing a portion or all of your initial investment if the company does poorly or the stock market drops in value. But you also may see the stock increase in value beyond what you could earn from the bonds. If you buy the stock, you become an "owner " of the company.

You wrestle with the decision. If you buy the bonds, you will get your money back plus the 8% interest a year. And you think the company will be able to honor its promise to you on the bonds because it has been in business for many years and doesn't look like it could go bankrupt. The company has a long history of making cars and you know that its stock has gone up in price by an average of 9% a year, plus it has typically paid stockholders a dividend of 3% from its profits each year.

THE MAIN DIFFERENCES BETWEEN STOCKS AND BONDS

Stocks	Bonds
If the company profits or is perceived as having strong potential, its stock may go up in value and pay dividends. You may make more money than from the bonds.	The company promises to return money plus interest.
Risk: The company may do poorly, and you'll lose a portion or all of your investment.	**Risk:** If the company goes bankrupt, your money may be lost. But if there is any money left, you will be paid before stockholders.

You take your time and make a careful decision. Only time will tell if you made the right choice. You'll keep a close eye on the company and keep the stock as long as the company keeps selling a quality car that consumers want to drive, and it can make an acceptable profit from its sales.

Why Some Investments Make Money and Others Don't

You can potentially make money in an investment if:

- The company performs better than its competitors.
- Other investors recognize it's a good company, so that when it comes time to sell your investment, others want to buy it.
- The company makes profits, meaning they make enough money to pay you interest for your bond, or maybe dividends on your stock.

You can lose money if:

- The company's competitors are better than it is.
- Consumers don't want to buy the company's products or services.
- The company's officers fail at managing the business well, they spend too much money, and their expenses are larger than their profits.
- Other investors that you would need to sell to think the company's stock is too expensive given its performance and future outlook.
- The people running the company are dishonest. They use your money to buy homes, clothes, and vacations, instead of using your money on the business.
- They lie about any aspect of the business: claim past or future profits that do not exist, claim it has contracts to sell its products when it doesn't, or make up fake numbers on their finances to dupe investors.
- The brokers who sell the company's stock manipulate the price so that it doesn't reflect the true value of the company. After they pump up the price, these brokers dump the stock, the price falls, and investors lose their money.
- For whatever reason, you have to sell your investment when the market is down.

Mutual Funds

Because it is sometimes hard for investors to become experts on various businesses—for example, what are the best steel, automobile, or telephone companies—investors often depend on professionals who are trained to investigate companies and recommend companies that are likely to succeed. Since it takes work to pick the stocks or bonds of the companies that have the best chance to do well in the future, many investors choose to invest in mutual funds.

What Is a Mutual Fund?

A mutual fund is a pool of money run by a professional or group of professionals called the "investment adviser." In a managed mutual fund, after investigating the prospects of many companies, the fund's investment adviser will pick the stocks or bonds of companies and put them into a fund.

Investors can buy shares of the fund, and their shares rise or fall in value as the values of the stocks and bonds in the fund rise and fall. Investors may typically pay a fee when they buy or sell their shares in the fund, and those fees in part pay the salaries and expenses of the professionals who manage the fund.

Even small fees can and do add up and eat into a significant chunk of the returns a mutual fund is likely to produce, so you need to look carefully at how much a fund costs and think about how much it will cost you over the amount of time you plan to own its shares. If two funds are similar in every way except that one charges a higher fee than the other, you'll make more money by choosing the fund with the lower annual costs.

For more information about mutual fund fees and expenses, be sure to read our brochure entitled "Invest Wisely:An Introduction to Mutual Funds"—which you can read online at **www.investor.gov** or order for free by calling the Federal Citizen Information Center at **(888) 878-3256**.

Mutual Funds without Active Management

One way that investors can obtain for themselves nearly the full returns of the market is to invest in an "index fund." This is a mutual fund that does not attempt to pick and choose stocks of individual companies based upon the research of the mutual fund managers or to try to time the market's movements. An index fund seeks to equal the returns of a major stock index, such as the Standard & Poor's 500, the Wilshire 5000, or the Russell 3000. Through computer programmed buying and selling, an index fund tracks the holdings of a chosen index, and so shows the same returns as an index minus, of course, the annual fees involved in running the fund. The fees for index mutual funds generally are much lower than the fees for managed mutual funds.

Historical data shows that index funds have, primarily because of their lower fees, enjoyed higher returns than the average managed mutual fund. But, like any investment, index funds involve risk.

Watch "Turnover" to Avoid Paying Excesstaxes

To maximize your mutual fund returns, or any investment returns, know the effect that taxes can have on what actually ends up in your pocket. Mutual funds that trade quickly in and out of stocks will have what is known as "high turnover." While selling a stock that has moved up in price does lock in a profit for the fund, this is a profit for which taxes have to be paid. Turnover in a fund creates taxable capital gains, which are paid by the mutual fund shareholders. All mutual funds are now mandated by the SEC to show both their before- and after-tax returns. The differences between what a fund is reportedly earning, and what a fund is earning after taxes are paid on the dividends and capital gains, can be quite striking. If you plan to hold mutual funds in a taxable account, be sure to check out these historical returns in the mutual fund prospectus to see what kind of taxes you might be likely to incur.

Do I Need an Investment Professional?

Are you the type of person who will read as much as possible about potential investments and ask questions about them? If so, maybe you don't need investment advice. But if you're busy with your job, your children, or other responsibilities, or feel you don't know enough about investing on your own, then you may need professional investment advice.

WARNING!
Before You Invest Always Check with the SEC and Your State's Securities Regulator:
Is the investment registered?
Have investors complained about the investment in the past?
Have the people who own or manage the investment been in trouble in the past?
Is the person selling me this investment licensed in my state?
Has that person been in trouble with the SEC, my state, or other investors in the past?

Investment professionals offer a variety of services at a variety of prices. It pays to comparison shop. You can get investment advice from most financial institutions that sell investments, including brokerages, banks, mutual funds, and insurance companies. You can also hire a broker, an investment adviser, an accountant, a financial planner, or other professional to help you make investment decisions.

Some financial planners and investment advisers offer a complete financial plan, assessing every aspect of your financial life and developing a detailed strategy for meeting your financial goals. They may charge you a fee for the plan, a percentage of your assets that they manage, or receive commissions from the companies whose products you buy, or a combination of these. You should know exactly what services you are getting and how much they will cost.

Remember, there is no such thing as a free lunch. Professional financial advisers do not perform their services as an act of charity. If they are working for you, they are getting paid for their efforts. Some of their fees are easier to see immediately than are others. But, in all cases, you should always feel free to ask questions about how and how much your adviser is being paid. And if the fee is quoted to you as a percentage, make sure that you understand what that translates to in dollars.

In contrast to investment advisers, brokers make recommendations about specific investments like stocks, bonds, or mutual funds. While taking into account your overall financial goals, brokers generally do not give you a detailed financial plan. Brokers are generally paid commissions when you buy or sell securities through them. If they sell you mutual funds make sure to ask questions about what fees are included in the mutual fund purchase.

Brokerages vary widely in the quantity and quality of the services they provide for customers. Some have large research staffs, large national operations, and are prepared to service almost any kind of financial transaction you may need. Others are small and may specialize in promoting investments in unproven and very risky companies. And there's everything else in between.

A **discount brokerage** charges lower fees and commissions for its services than what you'd pay at a full-service brokerage. But generally you have to research and choose investments by yourself. A **full-service brokerage** costs more, but the higher fees and commissions pay for a broker's investment advice based on that firm's research.

The best way to choose an investment professional is to start by asking your friends and colleagues who they recommend. Try to get several recommendations, and then meet with potential advisers face-to-face. Make sure you get along. Make sure you understand each other. After all, it's your money.

Opening a Brokerage Account

When you open a brokerage account, whether in person or online, you will typically be asked to sign a new account agreement. You should carefully review all the information in this agreement because it determines your legal rights regarding your account.

Do not sign the new account agreement unless you thoroughly understand it and agree with the terms and conditions it imposes on you. Do not rely on statements about your account that are not in this agreement. Ask for a copy of any account documentation prepared for you by your broker.

The broker should ask you about your investment goals and personal financial situation, including your income, net worth, investment experience, and how much risk you are willing to take on. Be honest. The broker relies on this information to determine which investments will best meet your investment goals and tolerance for risk. If a broker tries to sell you an investment before asking you these questions, that's a very bad sign. It signals that the broker has a greater interest in earning a commission than recommending an investment to you that meets your needs. The new account agreement requires that you make three critical decisions:

1. Who will make the final decisions about what you buy and sell in your account?

You will have the final say on investment decisions unless you give "discretionary authority" to your broker. Discretionary authority allows your broker to invest your money without consulting you about the price, the type of security, the amount, and when to buy or sell. Do not give discretionary authority to your broker without seriously considering the risks involved in turning control over your money to another person.

2. How will you pay for your investments?

Most investors maintain a "cash" account that requires payment in full for each security purchase. But if you open a "margin" account, you can buy securities by borrowing money from your broker for a portion of the purchase price. Be aware of the risks involved with buying stocks on margin. Beginning investors generally should not get started with a margin account. Make sure you understand how a margin account works, and what happens in the worst case scenario before you agree to buy on margin. Unlike other loans, like for a car or a home, that allow you to pay back a fixed amount every month, when you buy stocks on margin you can be faced with paying back the entire margin loan all at once if the price of the stock drops suddenly and dramatically. The firm has the authority to immediately sell any security in your account, without notice to you, to cover any shortfall resulting from a decline in the value of your securities. You may owe a substantial amount of money even after your securities are sold. The margin account agreement generally provides that the securities in your margin account may be lent out by the brokerage firm at any time without notice or compensation to you.

3. How much risk should you assume?

In a new account agreement, you must specify your overall investment objective in terms of risk. Categories of risk may have labels such as "income," "growth," or "aggressive growth." Be certain that you fully understand the distinctions among these terms, and be certain that the risk level you choose accurately reflects your age, experience and investment goals. Be sure that the investment products recommended to you reflect the category of risk you have selected.

When opening a new account, the brokerage firm may ask you to sign a legally binding contract to use the arbitration process to settle any future dispute between you and the firm or your sales representative. Signing this agreement means that you give up the right to sue your sales representative and firm in court.

HOW CAN I PROTECT MYSELF?

Ask Questions!

You can never ask a dumb question about your investments and the people who help you choose them, especially when it comes to how much you will be paying for any investment, both in upfront costs and ongoing management fees.

Here are some questions you should ask when choosing an investment professional or someone to help you:

- What training and experience do you have? How long have you been in business?

- What is your investment philosophy? Do you take a lot of risks or are you more concerned about the safety of my money?
- Describe your typical client. Can you provide me with references, the names of people who have invested with you for a long time?
- How do you get paid? By commission? Based on a percentage of assets you manage? Another method? Do you get paid more for selling your own firm's products?
- How much will it cost me in total to do business with you?

Your investment professional should understand your investment goals, whether you're saving to buy a home, paying for your children's education, or enjoying a comfortable retirement.

Your investment professional should ***also*** understand your tolerance for risk. That is, how much money can you afford to lose if the value of one of your investments declines? An investment professional has a duty to make sure that he or she only recommends investments that are suitable for you. That is, that the investment makes sense for you based on your other securities holdings, your financial situation, your means, and any other information that your investment professional thinks is important. The best investment professional is one who fully understands your objectives and matches investment recommendations to your goals. You'll want someone you can understand, because your investment professional should teach you about investing and the investment products.

How Should I Monitor My Investments?

Investing makes it possible for your money to work for you. In a sense, your money has become your employee, and that makes you the boss. You'll want to keep a close watch on how your employee, your money, is doing.

Some people like to look at the stock quotations every day to see how their investments have done. That's probably too often. You may get too caught up in the ups and downs of the "trading" value of your investment, and sell when its value goes down temporarily—even though the performance of the company is still stellar. Remember, you're in for the long haul.

Some people prefer to see how they're doing once a year. That's probably not often enough. What's best for you will most likely be somewhere in between, based on your goals and your investments.

But it's not enough to simply check an investment's performance. You should compare that performance against an index of similar investments over the same period of time to see if you are getting the proper returns for the amount of risk that you are assuming. You should also compare the fees and commissions that you're paying to what other investment professionals charge.

While you should monitor performance regularly, you should pay close attention ***every*** time you send your money somewhere else to work.

Every time you buy or sell an investment you will receive a confirmation slip from your broker. Make sure each trade was completed according to your instructions. Make sure the buying or selling price was what your broker quoted. And make sure the commissions or fees are what your broker said they would be.

IMPORTANT CONTACTS	
SEC	**NASAA**
100 F Street, N.E.	750 First Street, N.E., Suite 1140
Washington, D.C. 20549-0213	Washington, D.C. 20002
Toll-free: (800) SEC-0330	Phone: (202) 737-0900
Website: www.investor.gov	Website: www.nasaa.org

Watch out for unauthorized trades in your account. If you get a confirmation slip for a transaction that you didn't approve beforehand, call your broker. It may have been a mistake. If your broker refuses to correct it, put your complaint in writing and send it to the firm's compliance officer. Serious complaints should always be made in writing.

Remember, too, that if you rely on your investment professional for advice, he or she has an obligation to recommend investments that match your investment goals and tolerance for risk. Your investment professional should not be recommending trades simply to generate commissions. That's called "churning," and it's illegal.

How Can I Avoid Problems?

Choosing someone to help you with your investments is one of the most important investment decisions you will ever make. While most investment professionals are honest and hardworking, you must watch out for those few unscrupulous individuals. They can make your life's savings disappear in an instant.

Securities regulators and law enforcement officials can and do catch these criminals. But putting them in jail doesn't always get your money back. Too often, the money is gone. The good news is you can avoid potential problems by protecting yourself.

Let's say you've already met with several investment professionals based on recommendations from friends and others you trust, and you've found someone who clearly understands your investment objectives. Before you hire this person, you still have more homework.

Make sure the investment professional and her firm are registered with the SEC and licensed to do business in your state. And find out from your state's securities regulator whether the investment professional or her firm have ever been disciplined, or whether they have any complaints against them. You'll find contact information for securities regulators in the U.S. by visiting the website of the North American Securities Administrators Association (NASAA) at www.nasaa.org or by calling (202) 737-0900.

You should also find out as much as you can about any investments that your investment professional recommends.

First, make sure the investments are registered. Keep in mind, however, the mere fact that a company has registered and files reports with the SEC doesn't guarantee that the company will be a good investment.

Likewise, the fact that a company hasn't registered and doesn't file reports with the SEC doesn't mean the company is a fraud. Still, you may be asking for serious losses if, for instance, you invest in a small, thinly traded company that isn't widely known solely on the basis of what you may have read online. One simple phone call to your state regulator could prevent you from squandering your money on a scam.

Be wary of promises of quick profits, offers to share "inside information," and pressure to invest before you have an opportunity to investigate. These are all warning signs of fraud. Ask your investment professional for written materials and prospectuses, and read them before you invest. If you have questions, now is the time to ask.

- How will the investment make money?
- How is this investment consistent with my investment goals?
- What must happen for the investment to increase in value?
- What are the risks?
- Where can I get more information?

Finally, it's always a good idea to write down everything your investment professional tells you. Accurate notes will come in handy if ever there's a problem.

Some investments make money. Others lose money. That's natural, and that's why you need a diversified portfolio to minimize your risk. But if you lose money because you've been cheated, that's not natural, that's a problem.

Sometimes all it takes is a simple phone call to your investment professional to resolve a problem. Maybe there was an honest mistake that can be corrected. If talking to the investment professional doesn't resolve the problem, talk to the firm's manager, and write a letter to confirm your conversation. If that doesn't lead to a resolution, you may have to initiate private legal action. You may need to take action quickly because legal time limits for doing so vary. Your local bar association can provide referrals for attorneys who specialize in securities law.

At the same time, call or write to us and let us know what the problem was. Investor complaints are very important to the SEC. You may think you're the only one experiencing a problem, but typically, you're not alone. Sometimes it takes only one investor's complaint to trigger an investigation that exposes a bad broker or an illegal scheme. Complaints can be filed online with us by going to www.sec.gov/complaint.shtml.

INDEX

A

B

C

D

E

F

G

H

I

L

M

N

O

P